TRICKS OF THE FLOOR TRADER

TRICKS OF THE FLOOR TRADER

Insider Trading Techniques for the Off-the-Floor Trader

Neal T. Weintraub

IRWIN
Professional Publishing®
Chicago • London • Singapore

© Richard D. Irwin, a Times Mirror Higher Education Group, Inc. company, 1996

All rights reserved. No part of this publication may be reproduced, stored in a retrieval system, or transmitted, in any form, or by any means, electronic, mechanical, photocopying, recording, or otherwise, without the prior written permission of the publisher.

This publication is designed to provide accurate and authoritative information in regard to the subject matter covered. It is sold with the understanding that neither the author nor the publisher is engaged in rendering legal, accounting, or other professional service. If legal advice or other expert assistance is required, the services of a competent professional person should be sought.

From a Declaration of Principles jointly adopted by a Committee of the American Bar Association and a Committee of Publishers.

Irwin Professional Book Team

Publisher: *Wayne McGuirt*
Associate publisher: *Michael E. Desposito*
Executive editor: *Kevin Commins*
Marketing manager: *J. D. Kinney*
Managing editor: *Kevin Thornton*
Project editor: *Christina Thornton-Villagomez*
Production supervisor: *Laurie Kersch/Carol Klein*
Prepress buyer: *Jon Christopher*
Jacket designer: *Chip Butzko*
Compositor: *David Corona Design*
Typeface: *11/13 ITC Century Book*
Printer: *Buxton Skinner Printing Company*

Times Mirror
Higher Education Group

Library of Congress Cataloging-in-Publication Data

Weintraub, Neal.
    Tricks of the floor trader : insider trading techniques for the off-the floor trade/ Neal Weintraub.
    p.   cm.
    Includes index.
    ISBN 1-55738-913-6
    1. Insider trading in securities—United States. I. Title.
HG4910.W364   1996
332.64'273—dc20   95-44313

Printed in the United States of America
2 3 4 5 6 7 8 9 0 BS 2 1 0 9 8 7 6

This book is dedicated to my parents, their parents, and my brother Philip and sister Lynn.

Table of Contents

Foreword
xvi

Acknowledgements
xviii

Introduction
xx

PART 1

Tricks

Trick 1
Avoid Market Orders **3**

Trick 2
Knock Thrice **5**

Trick 3
Key Number Tactic for Day Traders **8**

Trick 4
When Bonds Close on the Daily Lows **11**

Trick 5
Opening Range Boomerang **12**

Trick 6
Using Newsletter Stops **13**

Trick 7
Buying Strength and Selling Weakness **15**

Trick 8
Spread Tactics **17**

Trick 9
Year to Date **19**

Trick 10
Spread Traders Know Where to Look **20**

Trick 11
Day Traders Buy the Dumps
and Sell the Humps 24

Trick 12
Buy a Leaper and Sell
a Creeper 25

Trick 13
%K Day Trade 26

Trick 14
False Breakouts Are Great
Trades 27

Trick 15
Point and Figure Charting...
"An Old Reliable in Day
Trading" 28

Trick 16
Best Money Management
Technique for Day
Trading 30

Trick 17
Neal's Trend Determination
Trick (What the Floor
Uses) 31

Trick 18
Trend Tactics 3 × 1
and 7 × 5 32

Trick 19
Weintraub Day Trade
Trick 34

Trick 20
Traders Have Their Own
Newsletters 37

Trick 21
Like a Vampire on a Baby 39

Trick 22
Commodities Limit Down 40

Trick 23
What's Up, Doc?—Or Don't Be
Misled by Percentages 41

Trick 24
May I Have Your Order? 43

Trick 25
No Edge, No Trade 45

Trick 26
When the Floor Is Selling
under the Price Quote 46

Trick 27
Before You Look South,
Look North 47

Trick 28
The 90/10 Strategy 49

Trick 29
And the 80/20 Strategy **51**

Trick 30
A Little Knowledge Goes a Long Way... **52**

Trick 31
Option Secret?... Hardly **54**

Trick 32
Two Are Better Than One **56**

PART 2
Tips

Tip 1
Using Stops to Catch a Falling Market **59**

Tip 2
Crossover Moving Averages **63**

Tip 3
First Notice Day Tactic **65**

Tip 4
Up Move Then a Pull Back—Adam's Entry Technique **67**

Tip 5
Fading the Government Report Tip **71**

Tip 6
Opinion Leader "Hitch Your Wagon to a Shooting Star" **75**

Tip 7
Are We Limit Up? **78**

Tip 8
Midmorning Mercenary **79**

Tip 9
Commitment of Traders Report—Your Tax Dollars at Work **80**

Tip 10
S&Ps Don't Lie **82**

Tip 11
Do Not Answer the Wrong Call **83**

Tip 12
Tuesday Tip **84**

Tip 13
Do Not RSVP Treasury Auctions **85**

Tip 14
When Currencies Gap Overnight **86**

Tip 15
Buy the Rumor Not Too Fast **87**

Tip 16
Measuring the Resistance **88**

Tip 17
Carrying Charge Strategy **89**

Tip 18
Trading without Stops **90**

Tip 19
Volatility Trading **92**

Tip 20
High Risk Option Tactic: For Futures Trading **94**

Tip 21
Best Day to Trade **95**

Tip 22
Opening Failure Trade **96**

Tip 23
The Rule of 72 **97**

Tip 24
Retracement Tip for Night Hawks **98**

Tip 25
Uptrender Trading for Stock Traders **99**

Tip 26
Stay Long Bonds over the Weekends Only If You Are a Heavy Hitter **101**

Tip 27
A Bull Market Has No Resistance **102**

Tip 28
Treasury Bond Futures Do Not Always Track Interest Rates **103**

Tip 29
The One Fundamental We All Forget **104**

Tip 30
5.3 Percent and Falling **105**

Tip 31
Don't Leave the Pit Unless You Are Flat **106**

Tip 32
Recognizing a Good Trade **107**

Tip 33
Good Traders Don't Need Reasons... but Bad Traders Do **108**

Tip 34
The Computer Does Not Know When You're Losing **109**

Tip 35
Be Smarter Than the Computer **110**

Tip 36
Eurodollars May Be the Place to Start **111**

Tip 37
What Do Traders Read Week after Week? **112**

Tip 38
Tactics Are Better Than Technical **113**

Tip 39
Capitalism for the Middle Class, Socialism for the Rich **114**

Tip 40
Healthy Leads to Wealthy **115**

Tip 41
The Matter of Setting Goals **116**

Tip 42
EEK! **117**

Tip 43
You Deserve a Break Today! **118**

Tip 44
The Ultimate Tip and It May Be Cruel **119**

Tip 45
Breakout Systems Worked Great from 1980–1991 **121**

Tip 46
Traders Abhor Buying a Monday Morning Gap Opening **122**

Tip 47
A Mini-Course in Options **123**

Tip 48
Your Broker Is Like a Trading Co-pilot **125**

PART 3
Traps

Timeout for Perspectives
127

Trap 1
10 to 30 Percent Pull Back—
Please Calculate **136**

Trap 2
Convincing Yourself
that There's Big Bucks
in Futures **138**

Trap 3
Hold On—but Know
When to Buy **139**

Trap 4
IPOs Take the Money
and Run **140**

Trap 5
Running Stops...Will
Generate False Indicators **141**

Trap 6
Political Turmoil, Don't
Bet Patriotic **143**

Trap 7
Attention Day Traders:
Gann Is Not Elvis **144**

Trap 8
"Goofy" Trading...or
Falling in Love with
Your Position **146**

Trap 9
Press the Market and You
May Be Taken to the
Cleaners **148**

Trap 10
When Traders Go
BONKERS **150**

Trap 11
Trading in a Vacuum **151**

Trap 12
Act in Haste, Repent
at Leisure **152**

Trap 13
Raider of the "Lost Motion" **154**

Trap 14
Systems Self-Destruct, Will Your Trading? **155**

Trap 15
Let's Just Watch It... Don't Kid Yourself **156**

Trap 16
The Traders Trap... Sinking in Quicksand **157**

Trap 17
Buy with Pride, Hold with Confidence (The Grizzly Trap) **158**

Trap 18
Today's Market Wizard Can Be Broke Tomorrow **159**

Trap 19
Futures Education... I'm So Broke, I Can't Pay Attention **160**

Trap 20
Getting Stuck in Charts **166**

Trap 21
No News: No Clue for Day Traders **168**

Trap 22
Don't Confuse a Good Trader with a Bull Market **169**

Trap 23
My Broker, My Son **170**

Trap 24
Tendencies Are Not Realities **171**

PART 4
Spreads

Spread 1
May Corn/March Corn **174**

Spread 2
December Corn/July Corn **175**

Spread 3
September Corn/
July Corn **176**

Spread 4
September Soybeans/May
Soybeans **178**

Spread 5
Buy February Hogs/Sell
April Hogs **180**

Spread 6
Buy Wheat/Sell Corn **181**

Spread 7
March Soybean Meal/July
Soybean Meal **182**

Spread 8
October Soybean Meal/August
Soybean Meal **183**

Spread 9
July Soybean Oil/March
Soybean Oil **184**

Spread 10
May Soybeans/May CBOT
Wheat **186**

Spread 11
November Soybeans/December
CBOT Wheat **188**

Spread 12
July Soybeans/July CBOT
Wheat **189**

Spread 13
Sell a Teenager **190**

Spread 14
June Live Cattle/August
Live Cattle **191**

Spread 15
June Live Cattle/October Live
Cattle **192**

Spread 16
June Live Hogs/April Live
Hogs **193**

Spread 17
April Live Cattle/April Live
Hogs **195**

Spread 18
April Live Cattle/April Feeder
Cattle **196**

Spread 19
June Live Cattle/May Feeder
Cattle **197**

Spread 20
August Live Cattle/August
Feeder Cattle **199**

Spread 21
June Deutsche Mark/June Swiss Franc **200**

Spread 22
December Treasury Bills/March Treasury Bills **201**

Spread 23
May Orange Juice/July Orange Juice **203**

Spread 24
July Cotton/December Cotton **204**

Spread 25
May Lumber/July Lumber **206**

Spread 26
The Platinum/Gold Spread Indicator for Bonds **207**

Spread 27
Well-Known Spread Charts **212**

PART 5
Tales from the Trenches

Floor Traders Unabashed Glossary
227

About the Author
235

Foreword

Let's face it, the real reason you are purchasing *Tricks of the Floor Trader* is to increase your profits in trading. But let's take a closer look at profits.

In a recent survey of public attitudes toward profits, the lack of correct information possessed by the public was brought into focus. More than half the respondents thought profits were in the range of 36 cents per dollar. Yet these same people said a fair profit would be 20 cents per dollar. How many traders make 20 percent on the dollar after costs are factored? In reality, profits above 12 percent a year are considered good in our industry. That means, year after year. Not a flash in the pan and down the tubes the next.

At the same time, there is a certain grudging admiration for traders in the belief that their profits are gained from inestimable resources and quick thinking. Yet, while traders say how you handle your losers is important, it is more important to handle your winners. Because that is what counts—the profits.

Neal Weintraub, the author, is not promoting another get rich system like "Formula Fortune." (I think that's in my gas tank.) Oh sure, if you lose you get the purchase price back. Big deal. What about the thousands of dollars that just disappeared in losing trades?

You see most system trading books actually force traders to take the easy winners and hang on to the losers to the point where they can never come back. This message though subtle at times is one of the most important statements this book conveys. If I were the publisher of this book, I would change the title to read "Common Sense Trading," but I guess that wouldn't sell.

"And speaking of selling," *Tricks of the Floor Trader* should sell for three times the amount, because Neal gives the perspective of a trader and computer trader—not a system promoter. Even the software he makes available for Trade Station is called a technique and not a system. Too bad you can't sit in on Neal's class at the Chicago Mercantile Exchange but this may very well be the closest many of us will ever get.

Maybe Neal's style is a bit irreverent and maybe he is a bit of a skeptic (his comments on Futures Education were too painfully true), but it's time to have a breath of fresh air and not another self-proclaimed Pied Piper of Hamelin taking the public down the primrose path.

After reviewing Neal's "Tales from the Trenches" section, I remember one story he did not include. And since I am a computer and technical trader, I would like to relate it now.

> *A fundamental trader and technical trader were watching the late evening news. A story appeared about a man preparing to jump off the roof of the Wrigley Building in Chicago.*
>
> *The fundamental trader bet the technical trader the man would not jump. And sure enough as the story concluded it was a false alarm. The fundamental trader felt guilty about winning the bet. "You know," he said, "I knew the guy wouldn't jump because I saw the story on the morning news."*
>
> *"Well, I saw the same story on the morning news too," said the technical trader. "But according to my charts, it was impossible for him not to jump on his second attempt."*

Finally, enjoy this book. Read it in sections. The *Tricks of the Floor Trader* is perfect for today's off-the-floor trader. I know. I use these tricks myself.

Pat Raffalovich
Vista Research and Trading, Inc.
Atlanta Georgia
Miami, Florida

Acknowledgements

It is well documented that the ancient Greeks, besides perfecting the sundial, used a water clock for an everyday timer. It certainly came in handy on cloudy days. Water clocks were used to limit arguments in courts. According to most experts, the arguments were limited to about six minutes of water flow.

Perhaps the Greeks knew that attention span only lasts about six minutes. So, in this book, I made sure that no Trick, Trap, or Tip takes longer than six minutes to read. While I acknowledge the Greeks for their six-minute rule, I also wish to acknowledge the many traders who shared their ideas and thoughts with me. This book contains many of their ideas.

My parents were particularly helpful as a sounding board for ideas and concepts. And, of course, special thanks to my mother for reading the business press and noting key articles. And thank goodness, she now won't have to ask me "How is the book coming?"

Many people ask me how I became interested in this field. Maybe it started when my grandmother bought me a savings bond, or when my grandfather told me stories about Bell & Howell. I can still recall at the age of 13 receiving shares of stock from my aunt and uncle, Pearl and Jack Kravit. It was some sort of mutual fund; I had no idea what a mutual fund was back in those days. I really wanted a baseball mitt. Nevertheless, it is impossible to grow up in Chicago and not hear about the financial exchanges on LaSalle Street and Wacker Drive. Like a magnet, these institutions draw people from all walks of life. While the markets can be rewarding, they can be merciless. The markets will uncover emotions in you that you forgot existed.

Yet it was the Education Department at the Chicago Mercantile Exchange that gave me the opportunity to teach and which piqued my interest in writing. Special thanks should also go to the education department for allowing me to work with such a fine and professional organization. DeBorah Lenchard, the director of the department, has an inordinate amount of patience with some of my unorthodox teaching styles. Ron, Phyllis, Nora, and Curt help round out an excellent education department. After my early seminars, it was Ira Epstein who sponsored my first national seminars in Chicago and Beverly Hills in 1987. I think of Ira as the Stan Kenton of commodities.

My stint as manager of Commodity Options at the Chicago Board of Trade was invaluable in allowing me to meet scores of entrepreneurs and traders who value being their own boss.

Although I teach computer trading, I am also a student. And I'm grateful to the staff at DePaul University and at the Henry George School of Economics. They are on the edge of innovative market ideas.

The cover of this book was photographed by Marc Schuman. Marc and I are not only good friends and skiing pals but share a common respect and regard for the market.

While many seminars believe in cramming people into a hotel room and flashing overheads, it was Sam Tennis and Pat Raffalovich at Vista Trading and Research who urged me to create software packages so traders could learn to trade from the comfort of their homes. The folks at Peregrine Financial Group fostered an atmosphere of trust and mutual respect during my research for this book. Russ, Connie, and Russ, Jr., provided me the freedom and office space for my research at the Chicago Mercantile Exchange.

Finally, I brought the concept of this book to many publishers, but it was Irwin Professional Publishing that decided to take a chance and get off the same beaten track of trading books and try something innovative. I sincerely hope you find the ideas . . . innovative.

Neal Weintraub

Introduction

Self-knowledge and self-mastery are the primary accomplishments of a trader. You cannot master the market until you master yourself. Traders know this. Speculators may not. In the Taoist view, individuals who are materially oriented—who identify themselves with their possessions—have no real purpose in the universe other than moving matter from one place to another. Materially oriented individuals cannot evolve intellectually, because their attachment teaches the mind to become fixed and unflowing. Thus, your trading and your ideas become firm and fixed and you are not open to new ideas. And you focus on the end not the means. We have all met people focused on making money and not doing a good or fair job.

Perhaps my uncle Joe said it best when he wrote these words in my eighth grade book:

As you go through life
No matter what the goal
Keep your eye upon the donut
And not upon the hole.

Focusing on the money and not on the trade and being out of step with the order of the market is what separates the public from traders. Trading is not a science. It is an art. In order to have a valid scientific theory it must have two components. It must explain and predict. Scientists can explain an eclipse of the sun and predict to the minute where and when the next one will occur.

When it comes to trading, people do a great job of explaining and a mediocre job of predicting. Most of the money we spend on market information is for the "prediction." Truly, if trading is an art, and many of the social sciences are, then we must be all the more wary of people claiming to be so-called trading scientists.

There are no Market Wizards, there are only great Money Managers.

Independence is vital to the trader. Traders know you cannot predict the future. You can only identify trends and know when to enter and exit the market. If there were a trader or system that could tell the future, no trader would take the other side of that trade. There is no wizard who is so powerful and so all knowing that he or she can scare other people out of trading. Nor is there a trading system or indicator so powerful that it scares other professional traders into paralysis.

You are a trader, a speculator, but not a gambler. You do not take shots. The public believes they can trade anything from baseball cards to bingo cards to be successful. However, a good trader knows this is not true. What made you a good real estate trader will not always transfer to the stock or mutual fund side of the ledger.

At many of our symposiums, people merely tell me they want to make big money in trading. This fuzzy approach often results in less than desirable trading results. Be realistic. Do you really think you can turn $25,000 into $2 million? I am shocked when I read ads that tell people they can learn to trade within three days. If that were true, why don't traders sell their computers and their seats worth over $450,000 and take these courses?

Please Take a Moment and Write How You Would Solve These Trading Situations

A. It's Sunday, July 4, and the Chicago Mercantile Exchange is closed on Monday for the long holiday in the United States. Globex, the computer trading mechanism used for overnight trading, is closed, also. You want to find out where all the foreign currencies are trading and you wish to place a trade.

What do you do?

1. Wait until Tuesday morning.

2. Trade the cash market.

3. Trade on Monday evening on Globex.

xxii   Tricks of the Floor Trader

B. The Chicago Board of Trade has shut down because of flooding. You have a substantial Bond position on. There is no way to trade in Chicago and you are concerned about your risk exposure.

What do you do?

C. Your Futures position has locked limit up and you are concerned about another limit up day. It is five minutes before the close.

What can you do?

D. Your broker wants you to liquidate a position before a report comes out. What strategy might be acceptable so you can trade through the report?

What will you do?

E. People tell you a market is very liquid and it is easy to get in and out of your trading position within a minimum of price skid.

How can you verify that this is true?

Planning, Techniques, and Access

Between the 14th and 17th of the month, a report, *Industrial Production and Capacity Utilization*, is released by the government. In advance of the report, some traders are taking positions and appear very confident. When the report is released, it is dead-on in terms of market expectations. In fact, most times, it seems traders know the real number in advance of the report.

How can traders anticipate this number with such accuracy?

The Answers Are Awaiting You as You Read, *Tricks of the Floor Trader.*

"Most Trades That Are Planned Are Not Executed. Most Executed Trades Are Not Planned."

Before we begin, first, let me compliment you. As an off-the-floor trader (at home) and a pit trader, I have the utmost respect for the off-the-floor trader. You truly are traders. You have an idea and you execute it. You do not wait for the "edge." You do not wait for market orders or look for stops. Many pit traders are really market makers. They merely buy at the bid and sell at the offer. It's like going to work; it's just a job.

However, there are floor traders who have direction and price ideas. Over the years, these traders have developed techniques for survival. Today's pit traders may not have a notebook computer in the palms of their hands, but they have access to price information and they react to it. They also have news all around them. Some of it is reliable, other times it may be a rumor.

Since floor traders account for 50 percent of the volume on the floor, wouldn't you be interested in the tactics and methods they use?

We Are Not Enemies. We Are Not Friends. We Are Traders.

However, we occupy different points in the trading arena. And the attitude necessary to make money is the same for the public as for the pit trader. We can learn from each other. Floor traders are incorporating computer technology in trading, and computer traders are beginning to understand the difference between the screen and the floor. Some of the tactics discussed here may be relevant to your style of trading. Others may merely be thought provoking. Try to integrate them into your technical toolbox. Who knows, you may start thinking like a floor trader.

The most difficult item for most traders to write is a trading plan well thought out. Tactics are based on trading strategy. As you read through these trading tactics, the strategy behind the trade should become apparent. At many of my seminars, I have noticed traders cringe when asked to write down their trading plan. This has proven to be a very difficult task.

However, when I mentioned certain trading techniques that traders used, I found that individual students would gravitate to those techniques. I thought, here at last might be a way to "back traders" into a plan. Maybe this is a "round about way" of developing a plan.

By concentrating on these tactics, I hope you will develop a trading plan and strategy that incorporates these trading ideas (Tactics).

But remember, treat every idea, guru, and indicator with a healthy dose of skepticism and doubt. Because in the end the laws of statistics, probability, and money management will decide your success. Just because you're riding the wave doesn't mean the next wave will carry you to the shore of success.

Part 1

Tricks

There are various ways of placing orders in the market. Each one is designed to fulfill a certain task. Placing orders is an integral part of trading tactics. Time and time again I notice traders saying merely buy at the market, sell at the market. By not thinking your order through, you are at the mercy of the trading pit.

The so-called pit trader really feeds off the tactical mistakes the public makes in placing orders. Traders in the pit love "market orders," because they can make the market. That can mean the difference between a winning or a losing day. Placing market orders is similar to going to an expensive restaurant and ordering lobster off a menu that lists market price, without asking what that price is. Unless you are placing a small order, exiting a trade, or trying to impress your date, get the bid and offer for the contract you are trading. The pit traders do not trade with each other. They need you!

Trick 1

Avoid Market Orders

Are You Using These Orders?

LIMIT ORDER Limit orders instruct the broker to fill the order at a specified price or at a better price. If you are buying, you cannot be filled higher than your specified price. If you are selling, you cannot be filled at a lower price. When giving this type of order you must specify a "limit" to your broker. This is the best order to use when entering a normal trading market.

CXL ORDER (CANCELLATION) An order to cancel instructs the broker to remove a previously entered order from his or her trading deck. This may also be called a "straight cancel." When a cancel order is delivered to the broker, both the cancel and the order being canceled must be returned to the order desk. CXL orders are given late in the day when the chances of being filled are slim or the risk/reward ratio may not be favorable.

CFO ORDER (CANCEL FORMER ORDER) This order does the work of two. It replaces the order already in the broker's deck with a new order. "Buy five APR FDR 7050 CFO 7040." This order is telling the broker to "Buy five April Feeder Cattle at 7050 and cancel the order to buy at 7040."

It is easy to mix up CXL and CFO orders. Professional traders will use CFO orders more frequently. The public usually cancels an order and then calls back later with a new order after evaluating the market. The professional has already evaluated the market.

MOC ORDER (MARKET ON CLOSE) This order instructs the broker to fill the order at the market close, which is the last several minutes of trade (this time period varies with the exchange, the pit, and the clearing firm). This order must be filled at a price that falls within the closing range. This is where the public gets "killed," because the order can be filled anywhere within the closing range. Closing ranges can have huge point spreads. It is no wonder that the pits are crowded at the close. It is not the local traders getting out. It is the traders waiting to join the "feeding frenzy" supplied by the public.

STOP LIMIT ORDER It is a stop order that becomes a limit order when and if the market reaches a designated price. Many traders use "stops" and not "stop limits." There is a big difference. When merely using a "stop," your order becomes a market order and you can be filled anywhere the broker can get a local trader in the pit to accommodate the trade. A trader wishing to purchase 1 Dec S&P when a price of 165.75 is reached could do the following: Buy 1 Dec S&P 165.75. Stop Limit 165.85. In this example, the broker is instructed to buy 1 Dec S&P when the price of 165.75 is reached, but not at a price above 165.85.

Trick 2

Knock Thrice

This technique is used by Futures traders waiting for the market to knock at least three times before answering. For example, if Bonds go up to 98.22 at least twice (within a nominal tolerance), and fall back, floor traders will wait. The third time up to the 98.22 area, the floor traders begin to buy. However, when this happens, a test of two times is usually enough to confirm a move. This same technique works on the down side of a market, too.

No matter what you have heard, a market is never too high to buy or too low to sell. The 1992–1993 Bond rally is one recent example of waiting for the double top, then the triple top, then the head and shoulders formation. Then, of course, the traders waited for the key reversal. As one trader said to me, "A key reversal is a good name for what can happen to your bank account."

What is the rationale for waiting three times? Usually, the public has their stops placed at certain locations. The public cannot manipulate the time sequence of a stop. They cannot say, "The second time up, get me out." So the first time out, we have the public. The second time, there may be action by funds or commercials. If this action persists, we know the move has credibility. The floor is joining the rally the third time. If you are still on the opposite side of this move, you will be left behind.

When the market gives you the opportunity for a fourth test of a support or resistance area, this is usually a gift trade, because generally enough strong hands are holding the commodity to take it through the area strongly the fourth time.

Part 1: Tricks

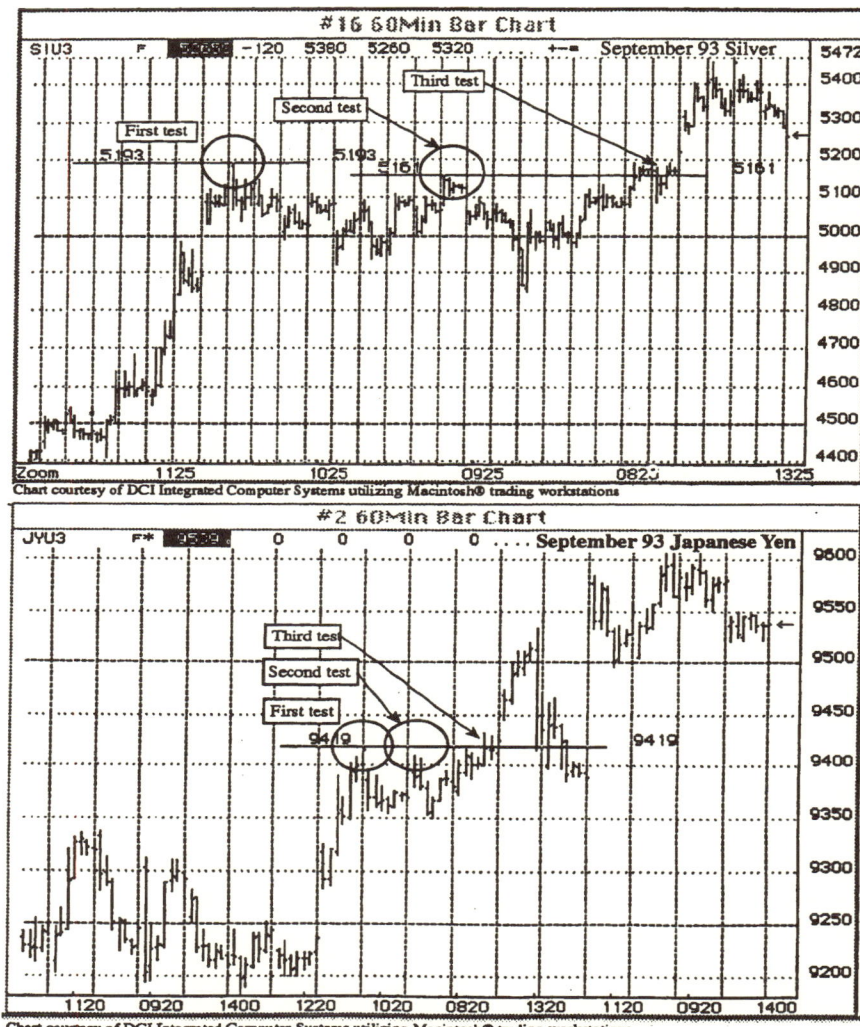

Example of Trading Trick #2

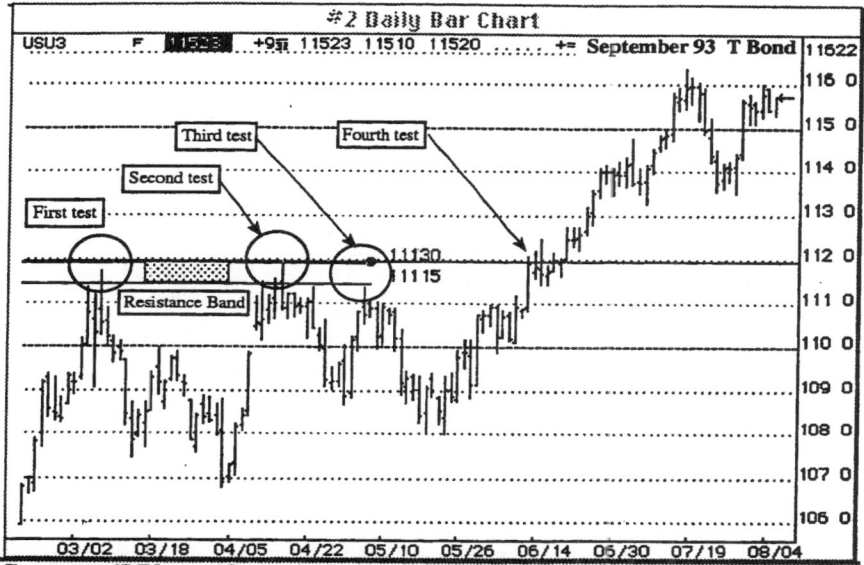

Example of Trading Trick #2 (4 is a Gift)

Trick 3

Key Number Tactic for Day Traders

Two minutes before a government report is released, jot down the price of the stock or commodity you plan on trading. This is more of a day trade technique, so the report should be anticipated by the market.

If there is a big move, wait until the market comes back to the number you jotted down. As the market moves closer to the number you wrote down, the floor will become more anxious. The number you wrote down is significant because it is a "pivot point." If the market moves through the number you wrote, simply go with the trend and risk the trade to where you entered.

Key Reports

When certain reports come out, floor traders look for a place to buy or sell. The following reports are a guide to the expected tactics you should anticipate from professional traders. They are not hard and fast rules, but a guide on how the disposition of the floor might be after a report is released.

Gross National Product	**Traders**
When the report is bullish,	Sell bonds.
When the report is bearish,	Buy bonds.
When the report is bullish,	Buy stock index.
When the report is bearish,	Sell stock index.

All other indicators provide information about Gross National Product.

Purchasing Managers Index | Traders
When this report is bullish, | Sell bonds.
When this report is bearish, | Buy bonds.

This index is not a government report but is published by the National Association of Purchasing Management. Do not relate the stock market to this index unless interest rates are going up. This report is difficult for the market to trade off. It is best to wait after the market has digested this report, since there are many components that must be analyzed. High-risk, low return trade.

Producer Price Index | Traders
When this report is bullish, | Sell bonds.
When this report is bearish, | Buy bonds.
When this report is bearish, | Buy stock market.

This monthly report is a "behind the scenes" look at inflation. It is the first indicator of inflation each month.

Consumer Price Index | Traders
When this report is bullish, | Sell bonds.
When this report is bearish, | Buy bonds.

Combining the double barrel of consumer prices and producer prices is vital for getting an accurate picture of the economy.

Chicago currency failure (as good as a key report)

This is used for traders in the evening and it requires access to a night trading desk. Wait for currencies to have a strong up move or down move. Closing at the extreme is the best. Now wait for Asia to start trading the market. If there is no follow through in Asia, go the opposite way of the U.S. move. This is a favorite trade for banks. Traders can take advantage of this trade by selling Currencies via Globex or the cash market. There are firms that will convert the cash market to Futures positions (EFP–Exchange for Physical) at the end of the day.

Trick 4

When Bonds Close on the Daily Lows

Sell the stock market. When Bonds close on the daily highs, buy the stock market. This is done after 2:00, CST. To be sure this situation works, wait and see if Bonds continue to worm their way up over at the Mid America Exchange. This tactic was given to me by my associates in the S&P pit. This technique works well if bonds have more than a 25 tick range.

Trick 5

Opening Range Boomerang

This approach to trading needs a little patience as well as floor access. First, determine the opening range of the market. Wait until the market comes back to that opening range. At this point, determine the direction of the opening range break out. When the market breaks out on the long side, you go long. If the market breaks out on the short side, you go short. This trade is short term and usually good for a three cent move in the grains and four or five ticks in the bond market. This is a type of scalping situation and should not be held for more than one hour. You will need to be in touch with the market on a continuous basis.

Example: At 9:30 A.M., soybeans open at $6.00 price level and drop down to $5.97. If the market returns to the opening range (6.00) you have the opportunity to trade. If the market moves up from the opening range by a cent, you enter the market immediately. Your objective is two or three cents. Under no circumstances can you allow any profit to turn into a loser when you are doing this trade. This trick is not for an effete trader.

Trick 6

Using Newsletter Stops

Many newsletter writers place stops so readers know how much "heat" to take on any one trade. Writers do not want to tell readers they missed a big move. And they do not want to risk more than 5 percent on any one trade. It is relatively easy to guess where the stops are placed. Usually, it is around the most recent highs or lows on a monthly basis. Traders at the exchanges have the opportunity to read most of these newsletters and note where the public places their market stops. Most writers use technical techniques without incorporating options or spreads. These have no staying power and are merely technical indicators. Rather than using the newsletter-writer's ideas on where to get out, use the newsletter-writer's stops as places to enter the market. The floor traders use the newsletter stops exactly that way. If you wonder how the floor knows where the stops are, chances are your favorite guru may be telling them.

The more popular newsletters are in the exchange libraries. Many traders will simply send their clerks down to read them and note the significant chart points. The prices of newsletters are in the thousands of dollars and they get quite specific in their recommendations. As a trader, it is difficult for you to invest this kind of money in such a speculative venture. But you can invest in newsletters that focus on your area of interest.

Never ever choose a newsletter stop over a money management stop. There are traders who are so punctilious that they gather newsletters from all over the world. But just because you are an assiduous reader will not substitute for experience.

THE BULLISH CONSENSUS Floor traders look forward to this newsletter because it usually measures how bullish or bearish the market is on any specific commodity. Readings over 75 are usually reason to consider going short and readings over 25 are signals to go long.

There are several rating services that rack the percentage of bulls and bears among advisors. The main rating services are Investors Intelligence *in the stock market and* Market Vane *in the futures market. Some advisors are very skilled at double talk. Editors of* Investors Intelligence *and* Market Vane *have plenty of experience pinning down such lizards. As long as the editor does the ratings, they remain consistent.* (Dr. Alexander Elders, *Trading as a Business*, published by John Wiley & Sons.)

The American Association of Individual Investors publishes a *Sentiment Survey* of individual investors. This is a great indicator to gauge the public's perception of the stock market. Survey results are available to members via an electronic bulletin board. Updated data are usually available by late afternoon on Friday.

I like *Ipso Facto* published by Doug Janson at Goldenberg-Heymeyer at the Chicago Board of Trade. Call (312) 929-1451 for a sample copy.

Trick 7

Buying Strength and Selling Weakness

It's true that some markets are stronger than others. Traders will simply buy the stronger commodity and sell the weak one. For example, if soybeans are up two cents and wheat is only up a quarter of a cent, you would buy beans and sell wheat. This day trade can many times turn into a long-term spread.

Contrary to some popular notions, spreading is not a risk-free procedure. Spreading does carry less risk than net long or net short positions. The extent of the price movement is usually different for one futures contract month than it is for another. In the final analysis, spreaders exist to make a profit on the basis of the differential between two or more contract months. There are more diverse views on the behavior of spread differentials than on the movements off markets. This can only encourage spread trading and enhance liquidity.

Frequently, the question comes up: Why should I even look at Spreads? Look at the difference between the price of Soybeans and the CRB Index.

Date	CRB	nearby Soybeans
02/12/93	202.25	570.5
02/19/93	203.1	573.25
02/26/93	203	577.25
01/19/93	213.90	586.75
07/23/93	218.99	727.50

As a Bond trader you may wish to follow the CRB for a hint of early warning inflation. Since Beans make up a portion of the CRB Index, it is a handy way to keep a perfunctory eye on inflation. If Beans make a dramatic move, you may want to consider selling Bonds. So, even the Spread watcher can use relationship trading for profitable trading.

About Floor Traders

Floor traders can take any side of your trade and know where to Spread it off. They know where the Spreads are trading. Does your screen resemble what we see on the floor? Or have you so rigged your own alchemy that only you understand?

Even if you do not trade spreads, it is important in your own trend analysis. A standardized value can be used to test the comparative strength or weakness of different commodities. The common statistic is called the "Momentum Oscillator %" and is derived from the Open, High, Low, and Close on either a daily or weekly basis. The indicator is calculated as follows:

$$\frac{(\text{High} - \text{Open}) + (\text{Close} - \text{Low})}{2 \times (\text{High} - \text{Low})} = \text{Momentum Oscillator \%}$$

This percentage value ranges between 0 and 100, indicating the relative strength behind the trend designation. The lower the number the stronger the down trend or the weaker the up trend. Consequently, the higher values for this indicator suggest more upward than downward momentum in the market. Values for this indicator reflecting 50 percent are to be viewed as neutral.

This technique is not limited to the Futures market. One could easily buy Apple stock and sell IBM stock in the same fashion.

Trick 8

Spread Tactics

Use a 23-day moving average for trading Spreads. You may draw it with a computer or keep a simple spread sheet. My associate, Steve Silverman, uses the 23-day average and trades with it.

When trading Grains, it is important to remember that carry exists when grain delivered for a future period trades at a premium to grain delivered to the spot or nearby contract. Inverted markets exist when nearby grain prices exceed those of deferred delivery periods. Whether a market is at a carry or an inverse depends on the interaction between available supplies, demand, and logistics.

A carry market usually indicates adequate supplies exist to meet current shipping needs, and buyers are willing to pay to have others store grain until it is needed. At a bare minimum, carry markets should cover interest costs. For example, at 8 percent interest, $6.00 soybeans would cost four cents per month interest to store. Because Spreads are so vital to your success, there is a special section about Spread techniques.

Part 1: *Tricks*

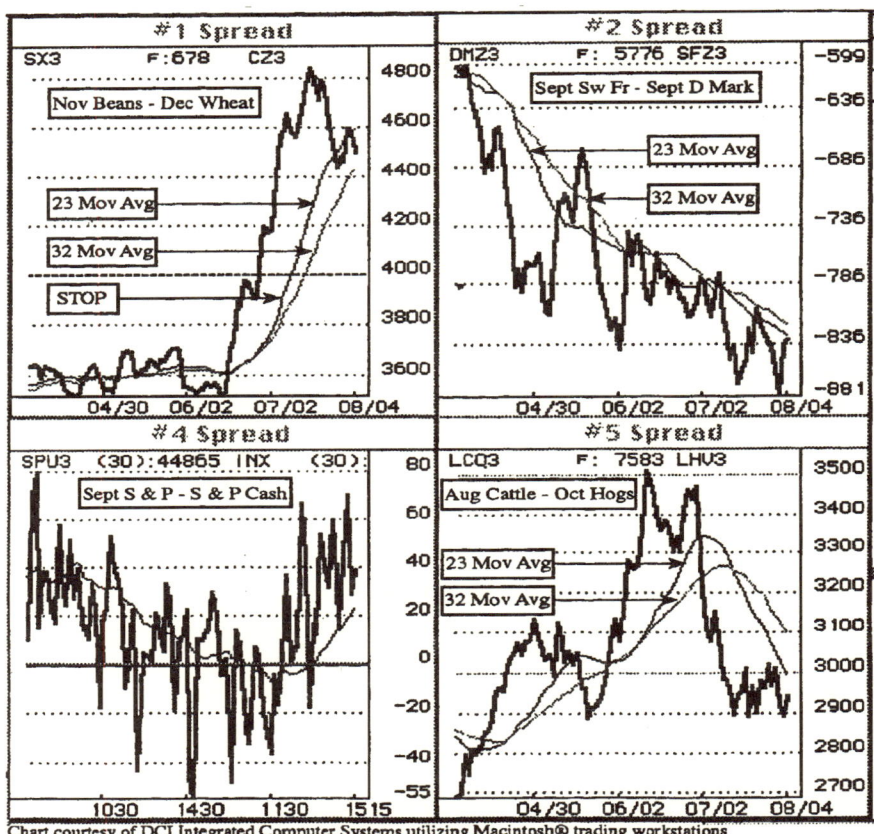

Spread Charts with Moving Averages

Trick 9

Year to Date

Most traders are aware of the price of a commodity, one year ago to the day. This is not because traders have a keen mind, but rather because it is posted on the trading floor. This gives the traders a good perspective on the market and avoids the tendency to get carried away with a one- or three-day move.

When a yearly high or yearly low is taken out, traders go with the move. Forget everything you've learned about support and resistance when it comes to taking out the yearly high or yearly low. Do not attempt to take on the floor. The world is filled with people who thought yearly highs and lows meant a move was over. Usually it is not. The importance of these numbers may appear evanescent to later generations of traders. But they do learn—witness the 1993 run up in Bond prices, or in Soybean prices.

Do not believe, if a market is trading below the cost of production, that the market must go to the cost of production. The market can anticipate changes in technology, lower production costs, government subsidies, and selling stockpiles. The reverse is also true.

Trick 10

Spread Traders Know Where to Look

Read the sentence below. Count the number of Fs.

Only count them once. Do not go back.

FINISHED FILES ARE THE RESULT OF YEARS OF SCIENTIFIC STUDY COMBINED WITH THE EXPERIENCE OF YEARS.

How many Fs did you find?

Did you count "OF" as a word?

Did you count at least six Fs?

Look again.

Did you miss any words with F?

Spread traders are always on the lookout for relationships. As stated in the example, traders are looking to buy strength and sell weakness.

Basic Types of Spreads

The interdelivery or intramarket

This is the most common spread you will trade. It consists of buying one month and selling another month of the same commodity.

The intercommodity spread

This involves buying one futures position and selling a futures month in a related commodity.

Merely because commodities are related does not mean movement is related. Cattle and Hogs are both part of the meat complex, yet hog farmers respond to an entire different set of supply/demand needs. Ask yourself, why am I doing an intercommodity Spread and is it a recognized relationship? The tendency to spread T-bonds against Soybeans is part of a new fad where computers merely play one commodity variable against another. It's being done by bored computer hackers, so the combinations are endless. Don't fall for Spreads that don't have any type of economic sense.

Professionals know the risk of trading commodities, and the strategy of using Spreads keeps the odds in their favor. Pit traders are many times forced to take a trade they don't want. They may be forced to buy soybeans, when they know the price will soon tumble. Because their job is take the other side of a trade the public trades. You are not forced to take the other side of a trade. Spreads are an area where you have historical data for your own use.

Even if you never trade an intercommodity spread, try to keep your eye on some of the various relationships.

Carrying charges

Carrying charge is the total cost to carry a product forward in time. For example, July Corn could and many times is carried to or stored until December. Carrying charges have three basic costs: storage, transportation, and financing.

Carrying charges are vital to traders because they determine the pricing relationships between now and the futures price. The NOW price is called the "SPOT" price. So carrying charges influence the price between spot and futures as well as of futures contracts of different maturities. One of the most significant charges in the futures market is the financing cost. That means, if gold costs $400.00 per ounce and the financing is 1 percent per month, the financing charge for carrying the gold would be $4.00 a month (1 percent × $400.00). You can easily see why the changes in interest rates can result in different carrying charges.

Limited risk

There are option spreads where you can limit the amount of money you may lose. However, one type of commodity spread has a theoretical limit on the distance it can go in one direction. When properly placed, it provides a good estimate of the potential downside risk you have in one direction. This is the concept we mean by limited risk.

Before you place an order, get the Bid and Offer for the Spread you are trading. In this way you have an idea of what the market is for your trade. The Chicago Board of Trade (CBOT) has Spread quotes posted near the price boards of the complex you are trading. Please do not subtract the two most recent prices from each other to determine the Spread.

Once you get filled at your price, chances are you will not be making a profit. That's because the floor got the so-called EDGE on your order. And because Spreads move slower, it may take a few hours, days, or weeks to make a profit. You can always ignore the BID/ASK and give your broker the price you want to do the Spread. In this way, you can wait for the price to come your way. However, there is no way of knowing for sure if it will happen.

Sometimes, the best way to get into a Spread trade is to set your price between the Bid/Offer. If the Bid is 6 and the Offer is 7, you do the trade at 6½ or 6¼.

The futures contract for the months closest to the nearby months usually trade at a discount to the back or deferred months. This reflects the cost of carry: the expenses of storage, interest, and insurance.

It is vital to your understanding of the market to know that, as a futures contract expires, the cash and futures prices tend to converge. Remember, even though many contracts are not delivered, they have real world application in terms of the real price commodity, and it may be and is frequently not the same price of the futures. Well, for one reason, geographical disparities in supply may exist. There may be transportation problems. There might be a problem with storage space. That's why futures traders get confused when they see a difference between cash and futures and expect them to be at the same price. It is the commercials and hedgers who see the disparity between cash and futures during spreading.

Many of the ideas we give you are based on the behavior of the cash and futures trading up to the point of delivery. You should be aware that historical data are kept by merchandisers to help take advantage of market disparities and make decisions about when to buy or sell the cash commodity.

Trick 11

Day Traders Buy the Dumps and Sell the Humps

And from Captain Nemo, do not diddle in the middle. This is an old Cattle Traders slo-gan. Selling Cattle over $80 and buying it around $65 has proved to be a high probability trade. While Cattle does not seem to catch the eye of many speculators, the above rule is something to keep in mind when prices trend. This slogan applies to other markets, if only to keep you out of a trading range market. My pedantic commodity research associates using overlays take seven pages in journals to state the advantages of buying dips and selling rallies.

Breakout traders

One of the great problems is whether to enter a market when it is going in your favor or wait for a reaction. Traders I know like to hop on the bandwagon. They will wait for Cattle to be up 50 points from a most recent low and then buy. They will wait for Beans to go up seven cents from a low and then buy. The more dramatic the low or high the more favorable for the trader.

On June 17, 1993, Soybeans opened nearly nine cents higher after being down for most of the week. It was the first up day from a low of 589 basis the November contract. Traders who bought the first breakout from the low saw Beans rise another eight cents for the day.

Currently, the Meat market at the Chicago Mercantile Exchange is not the most popular with the public. However, this market will react far less to overseas as well as to political events that occur overnight. While the currencies may give you more of a roller coaster ride, you may want to consider that the technical and fundamental indicators for the Meat complex are more stable.

Trick 12

Buy a Leaper and Sell a Creeper

A market that slowly grinds higher is a good buy. A market that soars is usually a good sell. From a practical standpoint, the 1993 stock market and bond market are examples of a market that keeps creeping higher. The bounding of the soybean market in 1993 is an example of a leaping market. The rationale behind this slogan is based on overexaggerated moves associated with overzealous public traders.

Trick 13

%K Day Trade

The following is a Day Trading tactic used by currency and S&P traders off the floor. You may note that the success of it is based on trading with the hourly trend, rather than fading it. You must have a computer with this technical study.

1. Wait for at least two hours of trading to commence. Be patient. Set an alarm if you must.
2. Look for a higher high or lower low after that range has been established.
3. Be sure there are no government reports to be released.
4. If you have a computer, set up a seven-minute bar chart.
5. Use your computer and buy when %K touches 20 and bounces up.
6. Sell when %K goes above 80 and breaks to the down side.

This technique is a variation of Kane's %K Hook that was featured in the May 1991 edition of the *Technical Traders Bulletin*. Try it and be sure you are trading in the direction of the daily trend. If this trade goes against you more than 40 minutes, then bail out.

Trick 14

False Breakouts Are Great Trades

After three days of up moves in a highly liquid commodity, the floor likes to sell the opening on the third day as the market opens higher. Usually, the people who are buying are undercapitalized public traders who see a breakout and wish to get aboard the rally. Look to be on the side of the floor trader for this kind of trade.

Tony Crabel, writing in *Technical Traders Bulletin*, has explored this type of trade. "The most basic patterns that I want to begin with are three-day patterns. You need three pieces of information from three days of trading:

"1. The day before yesterday is higher than the previous day's close(+).

"2. Yesterday's close is higher than the preceding day's close (+).

"3. Today's open is higher than yesterday's close(+)."

When this pattern occurs, the market is vulnerable to a selloff. When the market has a run like this, a higher opening is often followed by a decline. Mr. Crabel points out that, after a three-day run, the market is in a short-term overbought or oversold condition. He knows it takes a tremendous amount of pressure to move a market in the same direction for three days.

So the next time you see a market moving higher on the third day after the Opening, you may consider fading the move. But don't forget your Stop and be sure there is no report being released.

Trick 15

Point and Figure Charting... "An Old Reliable in Day Trading"

There are many trading techniques. One of the most popular is a simple point and figure chart. It is so popular that charts with grid lines are given free to floor traders. With so many unproved technical indicators around, I am amazed by the numbers of obdurate traders who refuse to consider this technique. The advantage of point and figure charting is its inherent ability to limit the amount of "heat" traders will take. For Bonds it is usually four to six ticks.

The construction of a point and figure chart is a simple process. As prices go up, Xs are plotted. When prices go down Os are recorded. As prices are rising, Xs are continually recorded in the same column. As it is becoming clear, the chart develops alternating columns of Xs and Os.

You may want to develop your own trading system. However, the reversal system or the Os must be defined. The most important item about point and figure charting is that you have the opportunity to know what is the long-term trend of a market. It is not uncommon to draw pivot points on the point and figure charts.

The construction of a point and figure chart is relatively simple. The difficult part is the correct size for each box and the reversal or trend size. Here are a few suggestions.

		Reversal
Corn	1	3
Beans	3	6
Bonds	4/32	13/32
Swiss franc	15	45
Gold	25	75
Hogs	20	65
Wheat	4	6
Yen	12	50

According to Amos Cohen, who teaches P and F charting at the Chicago Mercantile Exchange, the whipsawing process in point and figure has a true purpose:

Every reversal on the P&F chart in the area of distribution registers vacillations of hope and fear in the minds of those to whom risk is being transferred. How is this being done? Spreading, rumors, false price patterns. This whipsawing process generates the swings on the point and figure chart and measures the process of risk-transfer. The more swings the more time and money had to be reinvested on the part of the market to shake brave shorts and lure timid longs. For every greedy long or scared short that ran for cover, the producer established a short position. This process of shaking off becomes the measuring stick for the ensuing move.

Trick 16

Best Money Management Technique for Day Trading

First convert into dollars per contract the amount of distance from your entry price to the stop loss price you designed. Be sure it is a logical place for Stop Loss.

If the Stop Loss will chew up more than 2 percent of your equity, do not trade that market. It is too volatile for your trading portfolio. If your system will not trigger a major system reversal until 5 percent of your equity is gone, you had better get a different system or cut down the number of contracts or consider Spreads/Options.

Finally, let market action, not your financial condition, decide when you trade. Be sure you see a good trade not a whim. Remember the phrase, "Baby needs a new pair of shoes." It's used in the game of craps just before you roll the dice. Are you trading because you need a pair of designer gym shoes?

Keep your powder dry.

1. Open an account with as little money as possible.
2. Have the balance of your money in an interest account or a mutual fund that pays a dividend.

Trick 17

Neal's Trend Determination Trick— (What the Floor Uses)

Before you begin to trade, it is essential that you calculate the daily trend and the short-term trend. Assume today is Friday and the markets are closed for the week. The High, Low, and Close prices, together with the Pivot Point for the most recent seven trading days, are shown below.

Thur	Fri	Mon	Tues	Wed	Thur	Fri
high	high	high	high	high	high	high
50	65	45	20	20	25	35
low	low	low	low	low	low	low
30	40	25	10	5	15	15
close	close	close	close	close	close	close
40	45	35	15	5	20	25
pivot	**pivot**	**pivot**	**pivot**	**pivot**	**pivot**	**pivot**
40	50	35	15	10	20	25

The Pivot Point is (High+Low+Close) / 3.

Be sure you understand the concept of Pivot. It is a key number that you can buy or sell against. A more compact way of tracking the movement of the pivots is achieved by constructing another average, this time of the pivot points themselves.

Trick 18

Trend Tactics 3 × 1 and 7 × 5

From our experience, we have selected periods of three days and seven days as optimal. Depending on the commodities you trade and your own personal style, you may prefer other intervals. As long as you are consistent in your selection, we encourage you to try different periods until you find the ones suitable to your trading. Returning to our example, the first three-day average we can calculate is on Monday. This is the first day for which sufficient historical information is available.

After the close on Monday, we have pivot points of 40.50 and 35 for the last three days. Taking the average of these produces an average of 42 when rounded off. Remember, we divided all three numbers by 3. For the next day on Tuesday, the values of 50, 35, and 15 are used to produce an average of 33.33. This same technique is followed to produce the 3 × 1 value for each of the remaining days.

Day	Thur	Fri	Mon	Tues	Wed	Thur	Fri
High	50	65	4	20	20	25	35
Low	30	40	25	10	5	15	15
Close	40	45	35	15	5	20	25
Pivot	40	50	35	15	10	20	25
3 × 1 =			42	33	20	15	18
7 × 5 =							25

Here we have the same charts with the 3 × 1 numbers added. As a reminder, the 3 × 1 number is a three-day average updated each day. Note the 7 × 5. It is the high, low, and close of the week divided by three and it is calculated once a week. If the daily pivot is above the 3 × 1 or 7 × 5 and a commodity closes on its High, then the trend is considered positive regardless of whether the close is greater than the Open. Similarly, a Pivot below the 3 × 1 or 7 × 5 with a close equal to the Low signals as a negative trend condition. During the comparatively rare periods in which a market closes on its extreme, this aspect is viewed to be more significant than the relationship between the Open and Close.

The theory behind these methods is to smooth the daily fluctuations in the Pivot Points and begin to develop a sense of trend of the market. In the grid above, on Monday through Wednesday the Pivot is below the 3 × 1 number. This indicates a falling market condition. Similarly, the Pivot is above the 3 × 1 the rest of the week, implying the market has turned around and is now rising. The Pivot on Friday is the 7 × 5 level, at least hinting that the market is nearer to an average than it is to an extreme.

These are the same conclusions we drew previously, only now they are:

Daily Pivot	If above not applicable	Nontrending Market
Weekly	Weekly Pivot>7 × 5 and Weekly close >Weekly Open or Weekly close = Weekly High trend	up
	Weekly Pivot<7 × 5 and Weekly Close <Weekly Open or Weekly Close = Weekly Low trend	down
	If above not applicable	Nontrending

Trick 19

Weintraub Day Trade Trick

If the market is in an up trend and you are above the pivot, you are an aggressive buyer. As in any formula, care must be taken to look at what is going on in the market. That is why, in volatile markets, I will use the High + Low + Close + Opening/4 = Pivot V. The "V" represents volatile. In many cases, I will use the opening range. So in essence you are using four numbers to create an average Pivot and waiting for the market to Open so you may add the fourth number.

High + Low + Close + Open/4 = PIVOT V

- **For use in volatile markets only.**
- **Mainly used for day trading.**
- **Use for currency trading (the open is the day you are trading, and the high low and close are the previous day).**
- **Use for gap openings.**

The Pivot number is viewed as a balancing point: Prices above it are bullish and prices below it are bearish. The four support and resistance numbers that are sent to traders every morning via fax or wire service might be viewed as the trading envelope.

The formula follows for the four support and resistance number. Note Average and Support are same.

NAME	FORMULA	COMMENT
Pivot (Average)	(high + low + close)/3	
	(high + low + close)/4	add opening (average)
1st Resistance	(2 × Average) − Low	usually does not hold
1st Support	(2 × Average) − High	public buys here
2nd Resistance	Average − Next Low + Next High	breakout possible (Next Low as 1st Support)
2nd Support	Average − (Next High − Next Low)	watch for break (Next High as 1st Resistance)

Pivot Profits... Not So Easy... Here's Why

Having discussed the significance of the Pivot Average Point, it should be noted that while this number is useful in identifying daily buying or selling strength, it is subject to wide fluctuations in highly volatile markets. Because it is derived from prices for one day only, there is no direct correlation with longer time frames.

The moving averages serve to smooth the daily fluctuations in the Pivot Points and provide an indication of market trend. When the Pivot Points are above the moving averages a rising market is indicated (uptrend); conversely Pivot Points below the moving averages indicate a falling market (downtrend).

The premise behind the use of moving averages is that a trend once established is more likely to continue than to reverse. Therefore, trades taken in the direction of the moving average result in buying strength and selling weakness.

The advantages of using a moving average in trade selection:

(a) A trend-following technique is, by definition, objective. Variations can be back-tested to verify or optimize results.

(b) Because action points are well defined, uncertainty is minimized.

(c) By employing a trend-following method it is impossible for a move to occur without participation.

The disadvantages (or what traders won't tell you):

(a) Whipsaws are frequent and inevitable, and all signals acted upon are late by definition. That's why you must anticipate twenty-minute averages.

(b) Large numbers of long positions will be taken near the top of the range and short positions on weakness near the bottom. Since markets fluctuate in trading ranges most of the time, it seems clear that less than half of the trades will be successful. "Rules" developed in some markets will not work in others or even in the same markets during other periods. Attempts may be made to adapt the rules to volatility, but predicting volatility is no easier than any other kind of market prediction.

You now have the basics of a technique that traders pay over $800 to learn in Chicago.

The techniques are available on computer or fax by contacting Coz & Associates at 708-816-0798. Or Vista Trading at 404-565-3377.

20-Minute Day Trading Rule

When you are day trading and you have not seen any profit on your trade in 20 minutes and the price averages for each time are moving away from your mean price—Get Out by the Third 20-Minute Period.

A high is a high and a low is a low because the least amount of trading takes place at that level. Further, the Weintraub Day Trader is popular because the information is simple to get from the exchanges. In actual trading, the formula is calculated after the market is open and yesterday's low or high of the day has not been violated within the first 30 minutes of trading.

Trick 20

Traders Have Their Own Newsletters

Merely because a newsletter writer promotes sage advice does not mean professional traders really give it credence. The first thing a trader determines is the newsletter writer's credibility. Can he or she produce a statement demonstrating that actual trades are taking place in the account? Traders usually get ratings on newsletters from the *Hubert Newsletter*. While there is some disagreement on the best, the ones traders fade (take the opposite of their advice) include: *Your Window into the Futures; The Granville Market Letter; The Wall Street Letter; The Dines Letter; The Option Advisor; Commodity Trend Service*; most 900 number services; and Ken Robert's chart and phone service; plus anyone who sells lists of their subscribers.

You can always spot newsletters written by nontraders. Look for an intrepid, dauntless style punctuated with trading ideas presented in a bombastic way. These writers are nothing short of beguilers, and their picayune ideas are nothing more than trite and banal and vexatious.

At Goldenberg-Heymeyer, our newsletter writer and analyst Bob Lekberg spends over 10 hours a day preparing a grain commentary. It is not based on computer signals or moving averages, but rather on research, analysis, and careful reporting. Bob's letter is highly respected among grain traders and is faxed to traders and grain elevators. What's more, it is free to Goldenberg-Heymeyer clients. Another free newsletter is offered by the Federal Reserve Bank. No, the Fed is not always dry and academic. You may be surprised by the insight and sensitivity of the Fed. In a recent report, the Federal Reserve Bank of Cleveland stated:

> *Economic forces have enabled people to become materially more self-sufficient. In terms of what the average American*

can purchase, there is no denying that we have become a wealthy nation. For most of us, in many respects, this added wealth has enhanced the quality of life. Yet the perception that we have become a more alienated society exists. Wealth can be measured in different ways, and so on some of those terms the potential for further gains seems clear.

The best value for an overview of current newsletters is by contacting Consensus, Inc., and requesting a four-week trial subscription for about $25. Its toll free line is 1-800-383-1441. Now you won't take too long to winnow the true analysts from the pulp technicians.

Trick 21

Like a Vampire on a Baby

Very frequently, I receive messages from John Cruz at Spike Trading announcing the next move in the currencies. John is known as "the Count." I'm not sure if it's because he stays up all night or works in a trading room that resembles a Dracula movie. John came to Chicago from the Bronx. According to the "Cruzer," currency traders perceive a market top when new highs occur, which follows through with three consecutive lower lows. "Do not look for the market to take off," John notes. "When this happens I'm like a vampire on a baby." In trader language, if you are still in the market, you are John's next victim.

Another way to become John's victim is to forget that even during holidays the financial markets are open. And while you may be relaxing, certain brokerage firms are open and trading. On the morning of July 4, I received a call from global trader Ivana Bozjak at the Chicago Board of Trade. She was not only able to give me quotes but to make trades for international clients. So if John won't get you, maybe Ivana will.

Want to avoid being taken? Be sure you have access to a 24-hour trading desk. Why? Because no indicator in the world will get you out if you can't reach your broker.

Trick 22

Commodities Limit Down

The past always does not predict the future. But if the stock market sells off, it will drag Commodities down with it. Fund managers will trample over each other heading for the exits, and the locals will give bids that are ludicrous. Note that I said commodities. Currencies and financials may go in the opposite direction as people panic.

In times of crisis, people do not run out and buy soybeans. They may buy foreign currencies. Also, traders know a selloff in commodities can happen overnight and especially over a weekend.

Trick 23

What's Up, Doc?— Or Don't Be Misled by Percentages

Doc Leonard, a consultant and money raiser for various commodity trading advisors, posed the following: Trader A was down 50 percent in his fund last year. This year he is up 100 percent. Trader B was down 5 percent last year and up 25 percent this year. Which trader is doing better for the time period? Which one do you want to have trading your money? (Trader B has the better track record.)

Besides being wary of big percentages, use caution when examining historical trading models. Everyone who designed a model that seems to work should be retired. Only a few are. Don't kid yourself. The reason most system testing fails in real time is not the fault of the software but is usually the fault of evaluation methods, capitalization, money management, risk control, and fear. There just is something different about trading real money.

Doc has also commented about trading contests and winners. Contests and winners can be misleading. In short, percent return is a function of the capital used, time period involved, and market or markets followed. Most contest winners who then started a public fund have disappeared into obscurity.

Some brokers are notorious for touting a track record using contest results, unverified or unaudited results, or curve-fitted spreadsheets. Some even suggest that a one-week track record is enough to prove a system theory. Traders avoid this trap by demanding a CFTC/NFA disclosure document from a broker or the trader.

One caution: Even with Doc's years of experience, he freely admits it is still possible to be fooled. Floor traders are constantly being pursued by people claiming they have a system for trading.

For an accurate paper-trade test, I suggest entering orders through AUDITRACK. It's like a paper brokerage firm, except you don't erode your money. If you are thinking about buying software, get your vendor to supply AUDITRACK results. The firm may be contacted in Boca Raton, Florida.

Traders never believe a track record unless it is audited by someone else.

Trick 24

May I Have Your Order?

Unless you know what type of orders your exchange takes, you will continue losing money by initiating and exiting trades with market orders. With at least 14 variations, you can improve your odds of success referring to the chart below. Please note that the Chicago Mercantile Exchange will not accept a market open only. The Chicago Board of Trade will. Since the high or low of the day is often made during the opening, you may wish to temper your trading when dealing with different exchanges. (Special thanks to Jack Carl and Index for supplying me with this information in chart form.)

Until the computer becomes a reality at some exchanges, you can expect incredible delays as floor brokers get flooded with orders and take hours to give you a fill.

Types of Orders Accepted at Various Markets

Remember, many exchanges do not accept certain types of orders. Also, because any exchange may change its accepted orders from time to time without notice, it is wise to consult your order desk before placing unusual types of orders.

Type of Order

EXCHANGE & COMMODITY	LMT Limit	MKT Market	MOO Market on Open Only	MOC Market on Close	FOK Fill or Kill	STP Stop	S/L Stop Limit	SWL Stop With Limit	SCO Stop Close Only	SLCO Stop Limit Close Only	MIT Market If Touched	OCO Order Cancel Order	OBCO Or Better Close Only	OBOO Or Better Open Only
CME Chicago Mercantile Exchange — All Markets	Yes	Yes	No	Yes	Yes	Yes	Yes	Yes	Yes	Yes*	Yes	Yes	Yes*	Yes*
CBOT Chicago Board of Trade — All Markets	Yes	Yes	Yes	Yes	Yes	Yes	No	No	Yes	No	No	No	No	No
COMEX Commodity Exchange Inc. — All Markets	Yes	Yes	No	Yes	Yes	Yes	Yes	Yes	Yes	No	Yes	MOC	Yes	No
NYMEX New York Mercantile Exchange — All Markets	Yes	Yes	No	Yes	Yes	Yes	Yes	Yes	Yes	No	Yes	Yes	Yes	No
NYCE New York Cotton Exchange — Cotton / Orange Juice / Dollar Index	Yes / Yes / Yes	Yes / Yes / Yes	No / No / No	Yes / Yes / Yes	Yes / Yes / Yes	Yes / Yes / Yes	Yes* / Yes / Yes	Yes / Yes / Yes	Yes / Yes / Yes*	No / No / No	Yes / Yes* / Yes	Yes* / Yes* / Yes*	No / No / No	No / No / No
CSCE Coffee, Sugar, Cocoa Exchange — Coffee / Sugar / Cocoa	Yes / Yes / Yes	Yes / Yes / Yes	No / Yes / Yes	Yes / Yes / Yes	Yes / Yes / Yes	Yes / Yes / Yes	Yes / Yes / Yes	Yes / Yes / Yes	Yes / Yes / Yes	No / No / No	Yes / Yes / Yes	Yes* / Yes / Yes	No / No / No	No / No / No
NYFE New York Futures Exchange — All Markets	Yes	Yes	No	Yes	Yes	Yes	Yes	Yes	Yes	No	Yes	MOC	Yes	No
KCBT Kansas City Board of Trade — Value Line / Wheat	Yes / Yes	Yes / Yes	No / No	Yes / Yes	Yes / Yes	Yes / Yes	Yes / Yes	Yes / Yes	Yes / Yes	Yes / Yes	Yes / Yes	Yes / Yes	No / No	No / No
MID-AM Mid-America Commodity Exchange — All Markets	Yes	Yes	No	Yes	Yes	Yes	No	No	Yes	No	No	Yes**	No	No

* NOT HELD ** NOT ON?

Information contained herein is from sources generally considered to be reliable,; however, we make no guarantee, implied or explicit, as to its accuracy or completeness. Types of orders accepted at various commodity exchanges are subject to change without notice.

Trick 25

No Edge, No Trade

Floor traders make their money on the difference between the bid and ask price. That can be one tick or 10 ticks, depending on market conditions. As soon as they get into a trade, they have a theoretical profit. Usually, the price you want must be penetrated before you get filled. Add your commission, and you are behind the "eight ball." You may think you are a trader, but to the floor trader you are a public speculator. Know your limitations and appreciate the advantage the floor has. These traders have speed and location on their side. They spend all day in the pit. Savvy computer traders know the price on their screen is not the true pit price. Because the futures market is an auction market, traders get the bid and offer before placing their orders when they are off the floor.

If your screen says Bonds are 8815, and you say buy 50 at the market, what price do you think you will get? The floor did not trick you. You are merely receiving information 10 seconds later than the pit. This has nothing to do with your quote service. Your quote is late because it may not be immediately reported to the price reporter for 10 seconds.

Keeping with the bond quote, if Bonds tick up to 8817, you do not know if a few locals are covering shorts or a major institution is buying 1,000 contracts and bidding for more. Your quote screen does not tell you what is really going on. Understanding this will let you concentrate on trading, not on blaming "them" for bad fills.

Trick 26

When the Floor Is Selling under the Price Quote

It does not happen often. But when you start getting the world's greatest fills and the edge, watch out—especially when the market is rallying.

Recently, the price of Soybeans was $6.06. Floor traders were willing sellers at $6.05. That was an immediate one penny profit. Since traders are not known for their largess, I should have known a break was coming. And sure enough, my one penny profit turned into a three cent loss quicker than I could say Soybean.

Trick 27

Before You Look South, Look North

In my salad days, I visited Penny Davis in Winnipeg, Manitoba. Quick, where is Manitoba? Right, in Canada. In any case, during my visits I learned about the Winnipeg Grain Exchange and the vast agricultural resources of the prairie Provinces. What's so special about that? Let's explore this notion a bit further.

When our markets are closed due to a government holiday, the Canadian markets are open and extremely active. In fact, the entire world may be trading when we are on holiday. Unfortunately, most quote services do not bother to disseminate quotes on holidays. So the average public trader waits until Tuesday. The professional traders with positions do not wait—they act.

Recently, Chicago grain speculators were expecting rain over a three-day Memorial Day weekend. Additional rain, traders thought, would keep farmers from planting and, thereby, delay the crop. When the forecast turned dry by Monday, traders knew Beans, Corn, and Wheat would fall out of bed on Tuesday in Chicago. And fall they did. Beans went down nearly 27 cents and Wheat was down 12 cents.

Did the professional traders wait until Tuesday? Nope. They phoned their Canadian brokers, got the early grain call on Monday, and sold grains short on the Winnipeg Exchange. The old expression being a day late and a dollar short certainly applied to the Tuesday traders. Penny Davis went to work like millions of other Canadians and maybe phoned her broker when she learned that public traders in Chicago would be selling on Tuesday.

For more information on the Winnipeg Exchange, contact them at 500-360 Main Street, Winnipeg, Manitoba, Canada R3C-3Z4.

In a global economy, exchanges are worldwide. Avoid waiting for your broker and exchange to open while the rest of the world is trading and passing you by. In our computer trading courses we teach students how to access worldwide exchanges. If our students know, so should you.

Trick 28

The 90/10 Strategy

The Chicago Board of Trade is connected to the Chicago Board Options Exchange via a bridge that spans the city's elevated tracks. The 90/10 strategy is for conservative traders who may not appreciate the rancor and gyrations of the Futures market and wish to cross the tracks. Simply, traders place 10 percent of their fund in long purchased calls. The balance of the money usually is placed in a money market instrument. This instrument is not a futures product, it is an actual instrument, such as T-bills. The "trick" is to benefit from a favorable stock price while limiting the downside risk of the call premium by receiving interest on the money market instrument.

Let me quote from *Understanding Stock Options*, a pamphlet from CBOE:

> *Assume XYZ is trading at $60 per share. To purchase 100 shares of XYZ would require an investment of $6,000, all of which would be exposed to the risk of a price decline. To employ 90/10 strategy, you would buy a six-month XYZ 60 call. Assuming a premium of 6, the cost of the option would be $600. This purchase leaves you with $5,400 to invest in T-bills for six months. Assuming an interest rate of 10 percent and that the T-bill is held until maturity, the $5,400 would earn interest of $270 over the six-month period. The interest earned would effectively reduce the cost for the option to $330 ($600 premium minus $270 interest).*

Options are traded on the following U.S. exchanges: American Stock Exchange, Chicago Board Options Exchange, New York Stock Exchange, Pacific Stock Exchange, and the Philadelphia Stock Exchange. There are a myriad of option possibilities using interest income for investment purposes. They're worth exploring.

Traders can also use this strategy in a down market. Simply purchase Puts instead of Calls.

Trick 29

And the 80/20 Strategy

For every $1 you make trading, take $.20 cents of it and invest it in the most safe, secure non-Futures investment you can locate. In the last analysis, it's that 20 percent over a 10-year period that will determine your eventual success. Special thanks goes to Terry Dowling from Turner Financial Services for passing that trick on to me.

Trick 30

A Little Knowledge Goes a Long Way . . . Depending on When You Know It.

At one of my commodity seminars, I asked my brother Philip to speak and explain how news impacts Futures. His experience with national news networks makes him stand out in a world where people make judgments about the media, yet do not work in the field. What's more, since news does impact the markets, it is one fundamental that is respected but least understood. Phil's busy schedule along with family obligations prevent him from speaking at our seminars. However, he did ask his wife Sally and two lovely daughters Lynn and Laura for a few minutes on the family P.C. so he could contribute the following Trick. Somehow, I don't think he had to ask more than once.

The following trick is by Philip S. Weintraub:

The decisions you will make trading futures, commodities, or stocks should depend upon timely and accurate information. The question is not, Is the information available? Rather, What sources do you turn to for news that you will use as part of your successful trading strategies?

As a producer and writer for local and network news programs, I am made aware of major news stories that can affect the financial markets hours, and even minutes before the general public. However, that doesn't mean you are, too.

While working as a news writer for a network morning news program in the mid-1980s, I was made aware that a Liberian oil tanker was attacked by Iranian missiles in the Persian Gulf. The news reached my desk via computer and modem within minutes of the explosions. Minutes

Trick 30: *A Little Knowledge Goes a Long Way . . . Depending on When You Know It.* 53

later the Associated Press carried the news as well. The reporter was told to be ready for a live update from the Middle East.

Following the report, program executives were almost euphoric. They had scooped the competition. Unfortunately their bubble burst when they realized that, besides the East Coast, the other two-thirds of the nation never heard the report and wouldn't for another hour. Whether you watch "Today," "Good Morning America," or "CBS This Morning," unless you live on the East Coast you are seeing the program on a one-hour delay. That includes news reports, interviews, and weather segments. If you are holding positions that require quick, critical decisions, then watching TV, listening to the radio, reading The Wall Street Journal or other financial publications is the way to slow, painful, and agonizing financial death.

Trick 31

Option Secret? ... Hardly

Lately, books have been written about the great "Option Secret." Well, before you go and spend a fortune: The secret is *volatility skewing*. First of all, most options experience some type of volatility skewing. Look at it this way. In a "wild and crazy" bull market the public wants to buy cheap out of the money calls, hoping for a big move in the futures market. The so-called cheap options are actually more expensive since the public demands them. Volatility skewing is much like the guy who buys a used car for $15,000 because a new car is $17,500. Yes, the used car is cheaper but the new car is the better value. All the car buyer is looking at is price and not value. Whatever you do, never sell premium in options or sell naked options without a trading model that takes that into consideration. Traders who sell premium have some sort of volatility breakout system to cover option writing. The breakout model in many cases is not successful; it merely offsets the risk of writing options.

Philip York, of QBL Funds Management in Australia, puts it this way: "It is more important for a breakout system to be negatively correlated to the option writing than for it to be profitable in isolation."

Floor traders who sell premium will buy a higher or lower strike price for risk management. The ultimate sucker bet is selling calls and selling puts without any protection in the futures or option market. While it is true that most futures closing prices are within two standard deviations of the previous day's close, there is always the one-third that shocks the market. And if you purchase out of the money calls or puts from a broker, always ask what percentage includes your commission. What many traders forget is that low volatility may be the best time to purchase Futures—not when you read or hear about that commodity in the press.

Trick 31: *Option Secret? . . . Hardly*

Recently, I discovered the trading philosophy of Mauk & Randelhoff, a growing managed money firm in Duesseldorf, Germany. Over the past 21 months, its portfolio showed an incredible 291 percent gain. While most of the firm's trading is not shared with the public, I did learn that it tends to buy futures when volatility is low and it never adds to a winning position. Most positions are held over 120 days and winners are never allowed to become losing trades.

Trick 32

Two Are Better Than One

Straight to the point. Many traders have a primary and a secondary clearing firm. You should pick up on the concept and have accounts with two brokerage accounts. Phone lines go down, or your broker is not available, or you merely want to keep your broker on his or her toes. Jim Kelly, a broker for the Peregrine Financial Group in Chicago, states: "Brokers should assist with your execution and research and let you make the correct decision; comparing brokers is the best way of accomplishing that objective."

Part 2

Tips

On my trading bulletin board is a sign that reads:

Don't Extrapolate the Future

The subhead reads:

The absurdities of extrapolating trends in the future.

The sign reads:

"In 1960 there were 216 Elvis impersonators by unofficial count. In 1970 there were 2,400. By 1980 there were an estimated 6,300 Elvises and assuming continuation of the trend the number should hit 14,000 in 1992. By the year 2010 one in four people will be an Elvis impersonator."

As you read the following tips keep in mind that there is a difference between trader tips and trading tips. Avoid anyone who has a tip in the market.

In his book, *Elliott Wave Explained* (Chicago: Probus, 1992), Robert C. Beckman noted:

> *"The systems appear and disappear. The gurus rise like comets and burn themselves out like meteorites. With the arrival of every new guru and the appearance of each new method or system, investors in large numbers will accept the latest fad or fashion as finally offering the touchstone for unlimited wealth only to find bitter disappointment before long."*

Tip 1

Using Stops to Catch a Falling Market

The following technique is used by off-the-floor traders to catch an overbought or oversold market. Traders should try to capitalize on the fact that a quick and violent move to the upside can be overdone, and a correction soon may be at hand. Market swings are usually wide enough to accommodate the typical day trader. The idea is to follow a market up and then to get your order to sell filled as the market breaks in your direction. Most people think of using a stop loss order to eliminate a losing trade. This is the most common technique used in futures trading. However, it is possible to use a stop loss most advantageously to *enter a market* at an excellent price level.

Trading Example

On July 20 at 7:43 A.M. the Sept. D Mark was making new highs. I had no idea where it was going. But I can tell you that traders were getting chopped to pieces and losing out trying to pick the top of the market. I had made a few minor attempts to fade this mighty move only to get stopped out.

The D Mark was trading at 6823. According to my analysis, I knew if it broke support at around 6800 it could take a real nose dive. I called my floor broker and said, "Sell one Sept. D Mark on a sell stop at 6803. Four ticks DRT." That means, "Fill me only within four ticks of my stop, not any more." Well, the D Mark did break. My 6803 stop was filled at 6800. The market continued to break. I bought back my short position at 6686 at 10:48 A.M. This technique, "entering on a stop," should only be used in a highly *volatile* market. Breakouts should be anticipated from existing ranges. There is never any type of tacit understanding when it comes to stops. A stop becomes a market order. So do not think the floor will get only two or three ticks. It could be 50 or 100 points, depending on the market volatility at the time.

One service warns its subscribers to be extra careful when trading a "fast market."

When the gold and silver brokers determine there are "fast market" conditions, brokers can take all orders on a not held basis. Under their rules they have the right to fill any orders they want. Practically speaking, this normally means that losing trades are filled, but winning trades can disappear. The lesson here is to avoid using "the falling market" technique in fast markets.

When prices are changing rapidly, call the floor or your broker to determine if it is a fast market. When in doubt, stay out.

If you still are tempted to trade "fast markets," please read the following excerpt from regulation 320.16 of the Chicago Board of Trade regarding fast markets.

All prices in the range between those quoted immediately prior to and immediately following the "FAST" market designation are considered officially quoted whether or not such prices actually appear as trades on Exchange quotation displays and records.

TRADER'S COMMENT In a nutshell, this simply means that the price quotes you see are not valid in a "fast market." You can still be filled even though you never saw those prices on your home screen.

In low volatility markets, be a responsive trader. Let the market put you in the trade. If the Japanese yen is trading at 8934 and you believe it is a sell, let the market rally a bit to 8954 and then sell. It is vital to remember that Futures trading needs volatility.

A slow market will create slippage and grind out commissions. This becomes a moot point in a running market. Many times relatively cheap commissions can force you to overtrade slow choppy markets. Day Traders are especially guilty of trading this way—trading when there is no trade. Next time there is a slow day, do not trade. The floor traders certainly are not. So why are you? Look at your account statement. Is your broker making more than you? Could you pay off a vacation home with the commission you pay the broker? If your spouse saw the commission you pay your broker would he or she be jealous? Keep the answer to yourself.

When It Comes to Stock

Let the company make new highs and then buy. If you are wrong and there is no followthrough, you can certainly bail out.

Buying a new high in companies may seem like you are not picking a bottom. You are right. But there is a good chance that taking out a high may lead to even higher profits. One important aspect of the stock market is the human factor (psychology). Companies have people working for the increased profitability of the corporation. In the Futures market, there are traders, but they do not work everyday for the betterment of an entity or company. It is no wonder in a company, management is important to the overall success of the firm.

Caution: If a stock is making a new high and the key officers of the firm are selling, pass. Your broker can easily tell you what company insiders are doing, since it must be disclosed.

Unattended Positions Are Like Unattended Gardens

The market has a tendency to feed on unattended positions. If you do not pay attention to your positions, the market will. It is almost like having someone owe you money. If you do not remind that individual, you may never see your money again. An unattended position usually becomes a loss. Very seldom will it become a winner. That's why you must adjust your trading style to fit the amount of attention you can devote. Trading is an art, not a science, and should be treated as such. If it must occupy your entire life, ask yourself, Is it worthwhile? Trade the size and markets that are manageable for you. The next time you place a trade, ask yourself, How much time can I spend monitoring this trade? Perhaps you should consider placing that same trade as a Spread, as an Option, or in a Mutual Fund. Once you enter a position, be sure you place another stop to exit the position, just in case you are wrong. Your trading plan should also account for a profit objective. No position can afford to be left unattended. A simple STOP can make sure your garden is attended.

Support and Resistance: Charts as Optical Illusions

Drawing trend lines may be fun. But those trend lines represent real money. For nontechnical traders, trend lines are chart points drawn through recent highs and lows of a stock or commodity. They sometimes are drawn at 45 degree angles. When "gurus" say there is a lot of support 250 points lower, take out your calculator and decide if that kind of trade is worth it. Support and resistance are linguistic terms, but your money is not.

Is there a three to one risk/reward ratio in the trade you are considering? Many floor traders have the opportunity to trade any market they want. Why don't traders merely wander a few feet to the next trading pit and place trades. One reason is the risk/reward ratio. When you're looking at a chart pattern and put your stop at a chart point, calculate the risk in terms of real dollars.

Tip 2

Crossover Moving Averages

Day traders as well as long-term investors are very aware of moving average numbers. Crossovers of specific moving averages are usually what is being utilized by fund managers and various types of advisory services to assist clients in taking a longer viewpoint of the futures market. Unfortunately, these systems are sometimes a little slower than we would like them to be and give back considerable profits in nontrending markets or when the trend has ended. Floor traders are aware of these moving averages to alert them to overall fund positions in the market. This gives them the short-term edge in fading these signals. Floor traders are also aware of these exit points and will try to push the market lower searching for stops. Large funds cannot accept delivery and must either exit or roll their positions prior to first notice day.

Be aware when the three-day moving average crosses the 72-day moving average. Traders use the three-day crossing the 72-day as the main signal and the 33-day moving average as the trailing stop. In actual practice, you would place your buy when the three-day crosses the 72-day moving average. The 33-day moving average becomes your sell stop. Under no circumstances will day traders let a winner turn into a loser. If the trade is a loser by the end of the day, the trader must exit the position.

This is a great system to back-test. Remember, most funds are trend followers. You are going along with them. Floor traders take the other side of the trade and can do so because they pay less than $1 per trade. If funds are buying and commercials are buying, only a speculator would want to be in the way of this moving freight train. To hope for a system where you can outguess the funds is chimerical. The moving averages are your best bet. However, floor traders know that higher or lower market lows are more effective than moving averages for simple day trading. This little gem of knowledge is how floor traders keep track of anticipated trades by the large funds. Are we making lower lows? Are we making higher lows? Know the answers to these questions when you trade.

Tip 3

First Notice Day Tactic

This is also known as "first day of delivery" in the Futures market. Prices usually open lower and then rally on the first notice day. Many people have wondered why. Usually, it is because there are no weak longs. That means most speculative longs have been eliminated from the market. Most of the public are speculators. When first notice day arrives in a lead contract, the contract can be delivered. So all the stories you've heard about someone dumping beans on your lawn is a remote possibility. Seriously though, most brokers do not want to deal with customers who are long going into delivery. They will force you or highly encourage you to get out. From a percentage trade, being long on first notice day may be a good play. At least the odds are with you.

The question that is frequently asked is, Why can floor traders be long into delivery and not the public? The answer has to do with leverage. When the public purchases a futures contract they only put up a small percentage of the net worth. That means if they accept delivery they must post the full net worth of that contract. Since most public traders do not have that kind of money in their accounts, they exit the market. In short, leverage is OK as long as they do not have to post the entire amount.

Floor traders also trade on leverage. But if they decide to hold a contract into delivery they have made arrangements with their clearing firm or bank to lend them the money on the full net worth of the contract. That means they can borrow $1 million or even $10 million for a day or two on their signature. They only have to pay the interest on that money for the amount of time they are holding the contract. So they can borrow large sums of money for hours at a time.

So, while the public must liquidate, because they were over-leveraged, the floor trader may have anticipated the situation and had the banking connections to do it. You must deal with a broker who understands your trading style. Or if you wish to play this tactic, simply get long a contract a few days before first notice day.

Tip 4

Up Move Then a Pull Back—Adam's Entry Technique

This method needs a pull back based on using a series of bar charts. Simply wait for a trend. Identify it. Wait for a pull back. In a running market a five-minute bar chart will work. In a slower market utilize a 30-minute chart. You may also use a daily bar chart.

You enter the market when the market takes out the high of the previous bar. The real art is your order execution. Some people enter on a buy stop. The problem here is your fill. Entering on a stop is risky for a low percentage trade. Your stop must be placed near the low of the previous period. Execute this trade in a trending market. Limit your loss on these trades and try to go with the trend. When trading on the short side, this technique works well, especially when the public becomes complacent, buying dips over a period of time.

The scenario goes something like this:

Peter Public has been making money buying dips. So when the market drops the first time, he buys. When it drops the second time he buys that break, too. And to be sure he will not miss the third break; he buys that one, too. Peter is not trading anymore, he was the fourth break.

A money management stop or at least a break-even stop would have kept Peter in the game.

1. Determine the trend on a short-term basis.
2. Wait for a pull back on a five-minute or 30-minute bar chart.

3. Enter the market when it takes out the previous high for the most recent period. The opposite holds true when selling the market.

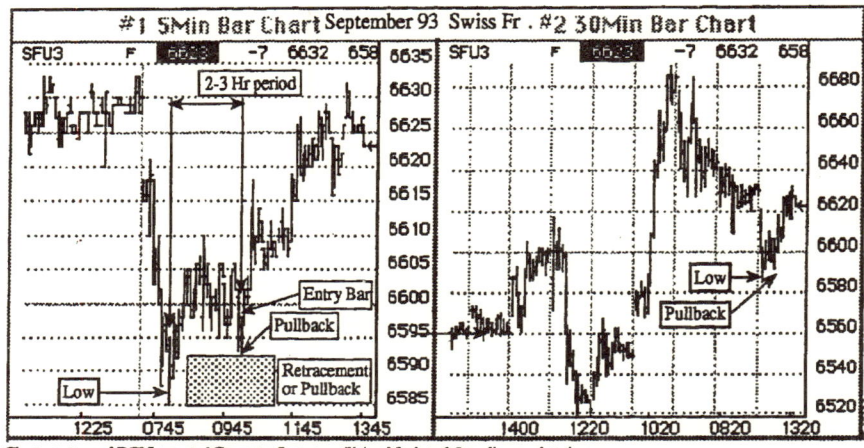

Example of Trading Tip Number 4.

Another way of entering the market was reviewed by Adam White in the "Technical Toolbox", a special monthly feature of the *Technical Traders Bulletin*. Here are the rules as reviewed by Adam White.

- *Of any four-bar pattern, if the third bar is the lowest low of the four, there is potential buy signal.*
- *Confirm that the lowest low occurs above a 27-bar moving average. If the low of the four-bar pattern is above the moving average, buy at the opening of the next bar.*
- *If the low of the four-bar pattern falls below the moving average, do not enter.*

   No entry strategy is perfect. It is possible to miss a good portion of very fast moving trends, the very trends we want to catch, if the trend moves so fast as to not permit a four bar correction to develop.

In honor of the author, I call this the "Adam technique." How does this technique compare to alternative entries that are more complex?

The most valid comparison might be to measure the Adam entry against traditional dual moving averages, where entries are made when a short moving average crosses a long moving average. This comparison is appropriate because the Adam and the dual moving average appear to be similar in nature. Research indicated that the Adam entry was superior. Following are Adam White's comments about the logic of this entry system. (*Floor traders use a variation of this system, but Adam's concepts explain the intuitive process that goes through a trader's mind.*)

The Adam entry method produces much better results because it follows the old adage of trading only in the direction of the generated trend. Most trends are a series of longer-term thrusts in the primary direction interrupted by short-term corrections of lesser magnitude in the other direction. It makes sense to play the main thrusts, not the corrections.

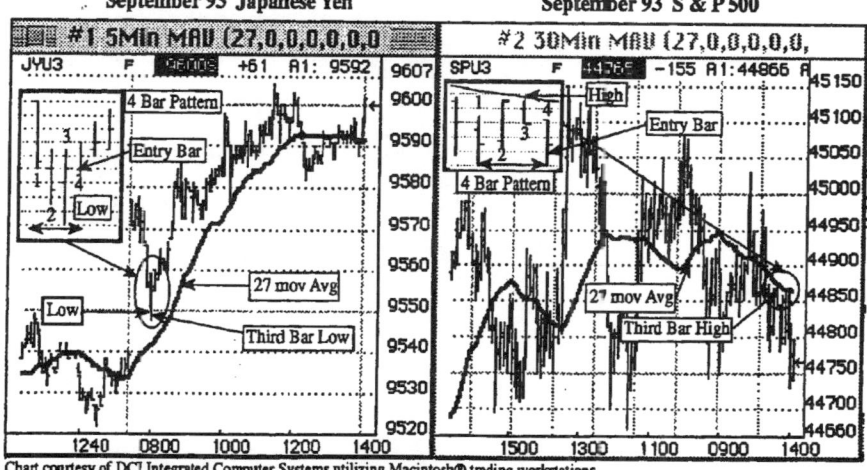

Chart courtesy of DCI Integrated Computer Systems utilizing Macintosh® trading workstations

Acceleration may also be a factor in the success of the Adam entry. It appears that the strongest trends would tend to have the mildest corrections. The mildest corrections are likely to bottom out on the near side of an adjacent moving average, so the Adam method is prone to trigger entries more often in strong trends. To elaborate, in the case of a rising trend, if the lowest low is above the moving average, then in all likelihood the thrust before the correction moved rapidly. An alternate would be that the correction that produced the lowest low was in itself rather mild. Both of these conditions are favorable for taking a long position as follows: We assume that significant trends are likely to follow significant initial thrusts, and that strong trends will have milder corrections than weak trends.

Review:

1. Of a four pattern, if the third bar (second from the right) is the lowest low of the four, there is a potential buy signal. Please note the word *potential*. You must wait for step No. 2.

2. Confirm that the lowest low occurs above a 27-bar moving average. If the low of the four-bar pattern is above the moving average, buy at the opening of the next bar. If that low of the four-bar pattern falls below the 27-bar moving average, do not enter.

Tip 5

Fading the Government Report Tip

When a key government report comes out and the analysts are anticipating a bullish report and the market reacts in the opposite way, you go in the direction of the market. So a bullish report that has a bearish reaction means you go with the market. This can also be used in a reverse situation. You simply go with the market. This may mean buying or selling at the market.

How to Trade It

When you are dealing with reports that come out after the market closes, simply place a buy stop or sell stop above or below that day's high or low. You must only allow the broker a few ticks' discretion, by using a stop order for market entry.

The following are two days of news commentary from DTN, a quote service commenting on the reaction to a *Cattle on Feed Report* in February 1993.

> *2/01/93*
>
> *The "report" fade worked to perfection today. Opening lows were never tested after the first 15 minutes and cattle futures gradually gained strength throughout the day. Feb and April contracts closed $0.75 and $0.45 higher, respectively.*
>
> *2/02/93*
>
> *Cattle futures jumped like "jack in the box" in the nearby contract Tuesday, as the Feb contract closed at 7942, up 117.*

As you can tell from the previous comments, the strategy, Fading the Report, resulted in over a 200-point profit. At this point, you would place a 50 point stop on your profit or at least take one-half of your contracts off. Never let winners turn into losers. Reports also can mean Treasury Auctions that are anticipated during the day. Or even a highly touted press conference.

What Really Moves Markets?

If you think markets do not turn on fundamental information, you are only using 50 percent of the tools at your disposal. This is not to say that government reports are fallacious. But rather, the news may be in the market. Also, be aware of news getting stale. In 1993, government reports indicated little or no inflation. However, the consumer price index for cereals was up 157 percent since the beginning of 1981, three times as much as the consumer price index for new cars. Consumers also saw a rise in diapers, drugs, cigarettes, and healthcare. While this news was slow to get out, the average consumer knew what was going on. So the old story of no inflation was looking a bit tired as Pa and Ma Kettle did their shopping. It was only a matter of time before the news got into the media and interest rates began to rise.

The clock is running out on the bogus no-inflation story. The American dollar is at an all-time low against the Japanese yen. The inflation clock is ready to chime. Be patient. Buy Puts and wait for the market to fall. It is only a matter of time and patience. Once the news hits the news show, it will be too late. You must anticipate the news. Fundamentals may not be the darling of the industry, but they are important in outlining a trading strategy.

There is a marked tendency for technicians to show examples—or should I say "cherry pick" the days—when a particular strategy worked and forget about the days when it did not. Fading the Report is not infallible. The prospect of a great loss is somewhat mitigated by the market placing you in the trade and your stop can be at the opening range. *Caution:* A "fast" market can play havoc with your fill, so be sure you give the broker a few ticks' discretion on your fill. I have seen currencies filled 100 points away when filled on a stop.

To Review This Strategy:

- Know the day and the closing prices the day before a report is to be released. (Obtain from exchanges or broker.)
- Find out what most analysts are anticipating. (Your broker can consult with you.)
- Place your stop above high or low of the day preceding the report's release.
- Enter the market on a stop and only allow a few ticks of discretion to the broker. Be sure your news is timely. Was it leaked or are you listening to a delayed broadcast? (In Chicago, "CNN News" is delayed 10 minutes on "WGN" and runs at 12:40 instead of 12:30.)
- Know if it is news or rumor.
- Check to see if news sources are giving predictions about the opening call for the next day.
- Have real-time quotes or be in touch with your broker on a 20-minute basis.

Why the Tactic Works

Fading the government report works for four reasons.

1. New information entering the market.
2. The delay between report preparation and release to the public.
3. You are relying on fundamental factors to outweigh the technical indicators.
4. Generally, the closer you are to a key government report the less important fundamental indicators become to large traders.

TRADER'S DISCUSSION On July 1 the USDA released its acreage report. It assumed no drop in total crop acreage from the

March report, based on weather in the Midwest for that month. Based on the report alone, the news was considered bearish, for the grain complex.

In fact, the *Chicago Tribune* stated on July 1:

Thursday's opening on the CBOT likely will see soybean prices drop 10 to 15 cents, according to Bryant, while George forecasts a decline of 10 to 20 cents a bushel. Despite the tighter supply picture for corn, both expect a soft opening of one to three cents lower.

What actually happened:

Corn closed over eight cents higher on the day and Soybeans closed over a nickel higher.

Tip 6

Opinion Leader
"Hitch Your Wagon
to a Shooting Star"

This is one of my favorite tactics. Opinion Leaders outmove the market by virtue of their comments. This can be a member of the Federal Reserve Bank or a member of a foreign government. For no reason, their very utterances can jump-start a market. Before you trade with an Opinion Leader it is important to know how well respected that individual is in the market place.

One current opinion leader is George Soros. He has no seat on the boards of the German Bundesbank or the Federal Reserve, but central bankers envy his power. In a period of three months his timely disclosures caused investments to increase. Mr. Soros stated his trading philosophy in a letter to the *Times* of London. Not having this information at a trader's disposal is a mistake. This is not to say that Mr. Soros's influence will not diminish. Yes, stardom is fleeting in this business. But a simple look at cause and effect should guide your reliance on opinion leaders.

Three examples of George Soros's influence include:

- Gold—he confirmed the purchase of Newmount Mining. The stock leaped from $3 to $45.
- Last June he formed a partnership with British Land. The price jumped 46 pence to 344 pence.
- On June 9 he writes the German mark will fall. The dollar gains more than one pfennig against the mark.

This news was not for insiders. It was there for any reader of a news service to discover. In this age of technicians, you may want to remember your old journalism courses. Not too long ago,

I met with a representative of the Bundesbank who was in the United States to check on the currency market. After a few brief conversations, I discovered his real motive was to figure out how the Bundesbank could capitalize on news stories or press conferences that originated out of Germany. If the Bundesbank was going to release news that was positive or negative to its currency, it wanted to reap the benefits of that news. Surprised? I certainly was. Governments taking positions in the Futures markets! Who would have thought of that 10 years ago?

How to Develop Opinion Leader Contacts

Let me point to the ways.

- Ask your broker who are the "movers and shakers" in the industry.
- Be sure they have credibility and are respected in the industry.
- Make sure the news is not acted upon before a major report.
- Read the *New York Times* financial section. Note who is quoted.
- Subscribe to a non-U.S. newspaper. I suggest the *Financial Times*.
- *The Wall Street Journal* is an excellent paper for developing a contrarian position. When that newspaper is bullish, you should consider being a bear.
- Realize the difference between a public relations piece and solid financial reporting.
- Do not ever—never—trade against the opinion of Dan Dorfman, a leading financial columnist.

- Write on your charts when fundamental news hits the market and separate that news into various categories, from government reports to rumors.
- Avoid opinion leaders who suggest doubling up on losing positions.
- Verify track records; ask for NFA audited track records from phone hotline gurus. Chances are they are really offering computer-simulated trades.
- Develop your own database of well-respected traders. Offer to exchange information with them via modem.

Tip 7

Are We Limit Up?

Most commodities have limits. That is the amount of price movement they can trade in one day. When a particular commodity opens limit up and begins to come off "unlock," you have a potential short sale. The floor has the advantage here, because they know how strong the bids are. If bids are weak, then the market will surely fall. When the market is "limit up," call your broker and find out how strong the bids are for that particular commodity. Most brokers can get that information. At any sign of weakness, or if the market is off limit for 30 or 40 minutes, get ready to sell.

Tip 8

Midmorning Mercenary

The market tends to pause at 10:30 A.M. in the Midwest. The direction in which it tends to drift usually points to the direction for the remainder of the day. By this time of the day, speculators have made their trades and the "battlefield" is set for the day. Many traders wish to wait and decide which side of the battle they will join. Much like a mercenary, they will fight for the side that pays them the most. Even they "love" to join the trend.

Mercenaries really have no allegiance or opinion. The public usually has more of an allegiance or conviction about a certain side of the market. While this is admirable, it is not the trading tactic professionals use. Once traders see the volume tapering off, they know the move for the day is almost over.

Various software packages do a good job of monitoring volume on an intraday basis. To be a mercenary, wait until the market makes a new high on lower volume and then join and "sell the market with both hands" (traders' expression). This can only be done when you are relatively sure that the move is over.

Traders will also examine the Liquidity Data Bank and get an idea of volume and price. And when all else fails, traders can always punch up the technical comments pages on the leading news services.

A more conservative approach is to be sure you are aware of all the short- and longer-term trends in the particular market. When a new high or low is made on higher volume, go with it.

Tip 9

Commitment of Traders Report—Your Tax Dollars at Work

This report is released twice a month by the government. It provides an idea of what positions are held by the various players in the market. Most traders look at the positions of small speculators. Frequently, they are on the wrong side of the market. Your broker should give you the results of these reports.

When Commercials are Long and Speculators are Short, go with the Commercials. If your trading system has you long the market and the commitment of traders reveals that commercials are short, consider buying Put options on your position.

There are other combinations. You can sell calls against your position or do ratio spreads. Remember the Sci-Fi television show where they used the phrase "yellow alert"? Commercial traders in the market are your yellow alert. A very powerful signal develops when fundamentals and the *Commitment of Traders Report* are pointing in the same direction.

This signal is often reported to traders:

Soybeans are sharply lower today . . . the fundamental traders are selling on a drier NWS 6–10 day forecast. Technical traders are selling because of the large speculative long positions shown in the Commitment of Traders Report, *as these numbers suggest there isn't much "fuel" for another rally. (Data Transmission Network Broadcast . . . August 26, 1993.)*

Clearly, a rally being propeled by speculators was an early warning signal to the market. In this case, the commercials were short and the public was long and wrong. When the market shows too many public traders are leaning one way, move your stop up, take your profit, or protect your position with options.

Tip 10

S&Ps Don't Lie

Jeff Jacobsen, a former S&P arbitrage trader and president of "Listen Only," warns traders that if the Dow Jones makes new highs and the S&Ps at the Chicago Mercantile Exchange do not follow, you have a potential short sale. Conversely, if the S&Ps rally and the Dow does not follow, go in the direction of the S&Ps.

Jeff also points out that 90 percent of the time, the S&P Futures contract goes back to unchanged sometime during the trading day. He suggests that zealous traders wait before taking an early buy or sell signal.

For more info on "Listen Only" contact Jeff at 312-648-3800.

Tip 11

Do Not Answer the Wrong Call

It is not uncommon for the news services to issue opening calls. Once in a while the market will open in the opposite direction of the opening call. Wait about three minutes after the opening and sell or buy in the direction the market is moving. Be sure it is in the direction of the market and not the wrong "opening call."

Thanks to Ben Cowell & Herman for this one.

Tip 12

Tuesday Tip

Prices tend to reverse Monday's gain on a Tuesday. If they do not, it may signal a new trend. The floor knows that many weak longs enter the market on Monday after newsletter recommendations are given to the public.

Dick Quiter, a broker/trader, is an expert at this technique. He may be contacted at 1-800-234-8540. Ask him for his "Tuesday Calls."

Tip 13

Do Not RSVP Treasury Auctions

My friend, James Szpila, a bond broker at the Chicago Board of Trade, warns that during Treasury Auctions the market is vulnerable to large swings (7–10 ticks at a clip) due to refunding. James points out that dealers are mainly hedging and technical considerations are not important. "I will not trade during these periods," notes Szpila.

James also watches the best and the brightest traders at the CBOT. He notices that they will not take more than five ticks of "heat" on a bond futures trade. And most are flat going into the Unemployment Number that is released the first Friday of the month. Most of James' public customers call directly to the Bond or Note pit. He is able to give them a feel of the market and remind them of these reports and auctions . . . and give them fills within one second.

Tip 14

When Currencies Gap Overnight

Go in the direction of the Gap. If the Swiss franc or any other currency gaps lower overnight and it is about to open lower on the Chicago Mercantile Exchange, look to trade in the direction of the gap. It is usually good for 15 or 25 points. If you must call in to get currency quotes and you are a short-term overnight currency trader, you are at a disadvantage. You are no longer a trader. You have joined the ranks of the public speculator.

My associates who run night trading desks have an expression: **No quotes—No clue.**

Tip 15

Buy the Rumor Not Too Fast

That is what the public thinks. What do the pros do? Sell, when company officials tell bad news to analysts first. Buy, when they tell good news to everyone.

Analysts are constantly calling corporations and asking how things are going. Analysts usually make revenue projections for clients and do not want to be proven wrong. They would rather revise an estimate than be wrong after company earnings come out. Recently B.J. Services Company, an oil and gas services concern, phoned analysts because it was not going to meet anticipated revenue estimates. The investors who got that bit of news sold at a good price. As for the rest of us, well, sorry, Charlie. According to the *New York Times*, the company believed it did nothing wrong and implied it would be more careful in the future.

Do you know the analysts at your brokerage firm? If not, start making a new friend.

Tip 16

Measuring the Resistance

This technique is used by traders and just takes a few seconds every morning. It is a handy way to measure resistance. The ratio measures the relative amount of contracts that changed hands relative to the daily range. As the ratio increases, you can assume traders were involved in the market. It should be noted that this is a subjective technique. Again, it is a little "tool" that floor traders like to use before the start of the trading day.

The Number of Contracts Traded (obtained from newspaper).

Divided by (High)—(Low) (done on a daily basis).

Tip 17

Carrying Charge Strategy

When you observe the various months on the price board of the Chicago Board of Trade, you will notice there are different prices for various months. The front month or the lead month is usually the contract that is traded most by the public. There is a strong tendency for the front month to gain on the more distant months. The hitch is to know when that happens.

Most of the time, traders wait for first notice day. This is when you enter the trade. There is a 77 percent chance for this type of trade to make money. But you must be aware that you may be delivered against. The problem you may have is with your broker. Usually, the broker is not cooperative in this type of strategy. It pays to have this type of strategy spelled out to your broker before you open an account. We know of brokers who will work this type of trade.

Tip 18

Trading without Stops

One reason speculators lose is that their stops get hit. And then the markets rally back to the original entry point. This is more prevalent in Futures than in stocks. But in either case it can prove to be frustrating. But when I see commercials trade big positions, I never see them place stops. No one ever says, "We hit the stops the commercials have in the market."

It is true commercials have a lot more money and own the product when they trade. You can trade just like a commercial. But you do it with options. You simply buy options when the commercials are buying futures and buy puts when commercials are selling futures. Please note this is the only time you should be trading without stops. Options are effective and not just for high rollers.

In the May 29 issue of the *New York Times:*

For conservative investors who toss and turn when their portfolios zing and sag, stock options can increase investment returns, bring stability to a portfolio, and maybe even result in a good night's sleep. Of course, options didn't get their dicey reputation without cause. Used speculatively or to control large blocks of stock, options can create huge losses if they force the investor to buy stock above market prices or to sell stock below the market. But, with interest rates on short-term, zero-risk Treasuries hovering around 3 percent, even conservative investors are tempted by the fees they can pocket by selling options.

When you trade in the Futures market, not only do you choose the direction of the market but you must be right in the price you choose to enter. Imagine, that all you must do is be accurate with the direction. In a "nutshell" that is the beauty of options. Now, you must be honest with yourself. If you enjoy the emotional swings of the market, then options are not for you. However, if you have a firm conviction about the market and feel the fundamentals are on your side, trading with options is one tactic that will let you ride out the rough seas of trading.

Tip 19

Volatility Trading

It is a fact that option volatility-based trading is more sophisticated than price-based trading. It does require more sophisticated tools (i.e., computer software). The most obvious kind of volatility-based trading is based on the observation that volatility, unlike prices, often tends to move within observable bounds. After moving to one extreme, volatility often returns, sometimes within a short time, to normal. Volatility trading does not require price forecasting skills. When you become a volatility trader, all you want to see happen is the price to simply move.

Options trading has been compared to playing 3-D chess. There are three dimensions you must be concerned about: price, time, and volatility.

Everyone is familiar with options in terms of price. This is the price game. When it comes to time, little can be said. We can put a strategy together based on time, but it is usually based on selling options. This leaves us with the concept of volatility. The ebb and flow of prices is what volatility trading is all about. Imagine the possibilities when all you want is prices to move or stay within a determined range. This will certainly open a new dimension of thinking about the markets.

Have you ever had this experience? You are long the soybean market and, being a good trader, you put in a stop loss. The market breaks, stops you out, and then soars just as you had expected. But you are not in the market. You were right in the long run but out of the market in the short run. Here's another example: The U.S. dollar looks as if it's bottomed. The problem is your charts are giving conflicting signals. You believe the market will move dramatically. The problem is, you are not sure which way it will move. Now you have some idea why we advocate volatility trading.

While we are on the subject of volatility, let's talk about the Mid Am Exchange. This exchange trades in smaller contracts. When the markets get volatile, the Mid Am will still allow you to participate in some dramatic moves. Maybe a 175-point move in the currency market makes more sense if you are playing for $6.25 a tick—rather than $12.50.

Another alternative is price averaging. However, the higher the price the more volatile the price action. However, there is one tip you should always remember:

Never, Ever Be Net Short Premium without Futures Protection or Stock Protection.

Tip 20

High Risk Option Tactic: For Futures Trading

This trade can only be done once. It can only be a day trade. It must be done in a highly liquid Futures market. Lumber does not qualify. Ready?

If a market is Limit Up for three consecutive days, Sell Calls on the opening of the fourth day. These calls should be Out of the Money Calls. If the trade goes against you for more than one hour, bail out.

Tip 21

Best Day to Trade

The best prices (lowest) are usually at the end of the month, and the highest prices are usually at the start. Most brokers eager to make commissions at the end of the month force prices down by suggesting to clients that they sell. This leads to lower prices.

At the beginning of the month, brokers call with great trading ideas that you cannot afford to miss.

Tip 22

Opening Failure Trade

This is a favorite floor trader technique. If the market fails to close above the opening range after one day of trading and it appears to be happening on the second day of trading, you sell the market. What do I mean by "appear"? Usually after two-thirds of the trading day has occurred and the market is still down and below the opening range, simply sell and risk back to the opening range. Traders consider the opening a validation of the previous day's close.

Tip 23

The Rule of 72

Traders use this handy rule for quick judgments when they are on the floor or do not have a calculator handy. The rule is a quick answer to how long it will take money to double. If you have an investment at 12 percent a year, it will take almost six years, 72 divided by 12, to double in value, a 100 percent return.

If a company says its earnings per share has doubled over the last 10 years, is that good? Divide 72 by 10 years and you get a ho-hum figure of 7.2 percent—the growth rate in earnings per share in percentage form.

Question: After all your expenses, how much a year do you make trading?

At that rate how long would it take you to double your money?

Now divide your time on an hourly rate. Like the results?

Tip 24

Retracement Tip for Nighthawks

During the night session at the Chicago Board of Trade, Bonds are traded quite actively. Since most of the time the night session is retraced during the day session, traders feel comfortable taking a position home from the night session.

This tactic can be used by off-the-floor traders who wish to trade at night and have some security they will be able to get out during the day session.

Tip 25

Uptrender Trading for Stock Traders

According to Jay Adler, a former S&P trader:

Trading system sell-signals are more likely to fail in the American stock market than buy-signals. That market is intrinsically an uptrending market and tends to outpace the inflation on a long-term basis. The stocks listed there employ people who work the value of their firms higher. This contrasts with commodities whose market's price lacks the benefit of employee labor. Asset building and project growth cause the demand for stock to exceed its supply over time. Since time gives labor the chance to work, time favors higher stock valuations.

Jay believes that to trade profitably *it is not necessary* for both buy and sell signals to work. One-sided trading systems offer ample profit potential, provided that a complementary trading strategy is used to auto-enhance the trading. It certainly can be argued that the American stock market generally rallies further than it breaks and, therefore, triggers sell signals more readily than buy signals.

1. Arm the buy side and protect against sell signals by establishing a bullish position first.

2. Use sell signals to offset or hedge against all or part of your bullish position.

3. If you completely offset your bullish position and the signal fails and the market rallies, you lose.

4. You are either long the market, hedged, or have a portion of your market position hedged.

5. Essentially you are trading with the long-term trend of the market that had been up.
6. You are most likely using options for downside protection when you get a sell signal.

TRADER'S DISCUSSION! Check the rally:

Supply or demand rally

In a bull market, a market going up based on perceptions of supply will fail. A market based on demand has the most potential for big profits. Is the market going up based on supply or demand? Demand must come from commercials or end users. Without them the public will fuel a rally and that eventually will fizzle.

Weather rally

If weather sparked a rally, it can also end it. When you are trading a weather market, factor fundamentals into your technical analysis. The trend is not your friend, the weekend forecast is. The most important factor in weather-related trading is the "240 Prog." The "Prog" is perhaps watched more by traders than current weather conditions as decisions on buying or selling. The "240 Prog" is a weather map produced by the National Meteorological Center for broad-scale atmospheric patterns in the next 10 days. (10 days × 24 hrs/day = 240 hours.)

Tip 26

Stay Long Bonds over the Weekends Only If You Are a Heavy Hitter

As long as the United States is a world power, any economic problem will cause investors to seek safety behind America's military might. That is usually done through Bonds or other such Treasury instruments. Weekends have proved to be important turning points for catastrophe. Insiders usually know about these events before they happen. Connections with the military and foreign offices are beyond the scope of most technical traders. The best bet is to strap on your Treasury Safety Belt for weekend rides. Options are the safe bet here.

Tip 27

A Bull Market Has No Resistance

And a Bear Market has no Support. My friend Bill Eng, who writes about day trading, frequently makes this remark at seminars. Traders know this, and the public is frequently tricked by selling strong rallies and buying big breaks when the rest of the world is going the opposite way. If the market you are trading takes out a monthly high or low, don't go in the opposite direction.

Tip 28

Treasury Bond Futures Do Not Always Track Interest Rates

Fact: Cash bonds and the futures at the Chicago Board of Trade move at different speeds. However, at delivery time the cheapest to deliver issue and the futures contract will converge to the same price. Remember, the futures contract is not an index that is weighted to issues in the spot market. The contract is a good mirror of the basket of deliverable types of Treasury issues. If you are a futures trader and especially a speculator, don't be thrown off by publicity that negates the importance of this contract as a useful hedging vehicle and yield curve indicator. Firms wishing to hedge can move the Futures market over a basis point. It is easy to get fooled in this market when hedgers have something to do and your technical indicators point you in the wrong direction. **Bonds overshoot, rather than react smoothly, to economic fundamentals.**

You will hear many traders talk about the T-bill Eurodollar (TED) spread. This is a traditional direction of rate trade. Eurodollars are not guaranteed by any government body, so investors in these instruments demand a higher interest rate, compared to T-bills, which are government-guaranteed instruments. Since 1984, when the Federal Reserve abolished maximum deposit rates, the yield spread between cash T-bills and Eurodollars has averaged 7.6 percent.

Traders know that when short-term rates are rising, the TED spread should widen.

Tip 29

The One Fundamental We All Forget

For a long-term look at where the economy is going, simply look at the price of real estate and land. And the amount of taxes levied on real estate.

Besides government reports and housing news, the relationship of land to the health of the overall economy is crucial. The idea of land and wealth has been around for over a century.

During the nineteenth century the United States witnessed a huge increase in wealth-producing power. People naturally expected labor-saving inventions to lessen toil and to improve working conditions for all—that the enormous increase in wealth-producing power would wipe out poverty forever.

As we now enter the twenty-first century, the same problems will be exacerbated. After falling in the 1960s, poverty is now greater than it was in the 1970s.

Paying farmers not to plant, taxing property improvements, and taxing buildings, rather than land, will certainly be salient issues in the years ahead. The great gauge of inflation is really the price of real estate. Blaming labor for high prices instead of keeping a watchful eye on real estate can be a mistake.

Here in Chicago, the Henry George School offers courses and tapes for people wishing a firmer grasp of economic fundamentals and the relationship of land to wealth. The school may be contacted at: 1772 W. Greenleaf, Chicago, Illinois 60626, ph. (312) 338-6698.

Tip 30

5.3 Percent and Falling

If the unemployment rate falls below 5.3 percent, you can bet inflation is just around the corner. Traders know the Fed is relentless when it comes to fighting inflation. Expect higher commodity prices.

Tip 31

Don't Leave the Pit Unless You Are Flat

Floor traders do not leave the trading pits unless they have no position. Or unless the buys and sells are even or spread. The rule was told to traders over 20 years ago. The updated version might read: Don't turn off your computer unless you close out your position. Or have a stop loss that will take you out.

Tip 32

Recognizing a Good Trade

What would you rather have? One thousand dollars paid to you for the next 35 days or a penny doubled for 35 days?

If you said the thousand dollars, then you'd better think twice before making trade. After 35 days the penny doubled becomes $343,587,383.60.

Day Trading does not mean trading every single day. It means being prepared to act on a good trade day or night. And holding it for maybe years.

Tip 33

Good Trades Don't Need Reasons . . . but Bad Trades Do

When the market is going your way, you don't care why. When you are losing, you need an excuse, a reason. Research directors play that role nicely. They supply reasons to the public why they lost. The logic can be a hotline or a leather-bound report. Brokers love to blame the research department for losing trades. So what's the answer?

Do your research before you trade. If you are wrong, get out. Don't waste your emotional energy looking for the "why." Your broker may lend you a shoulder to cry on, but don't expect more sympathy unless you keep trading.

In the book *The Art of War* (Sun Tzu. Ed. by James Clavell, New York: Delacorte, 1983) it states, "The general who wins a battle makes calculations in his temple before the battle is fought. The general who loses a battle makes but few calculations beforehand. Thus, do many calculations lead to victory, and few calculations to defeat."

Tip 34

The Computer Does Not Know When You're Losing

In pit trading, the guy you traded with knows if you lost or won on that trade. There is no hiding. No excuses. No time and sales. After three losers in a row, most traders take a break. When you are trading at your computer, take a break after three losers. Pretend the guys in the pit are there. It's a little tip that may save your trading day.

Tip 35

Be Smarter Than the Computer

Most people are. They are just afraid of the computer. At one of our first computer trading seminars done with Apple Computer, I invited Mr. Bernard Golbus. He recently had had a stroke and I thought for sure he would not attend. Yet, one of the first people there was Mr. Golbus. Not only did he participate but later purchased a computer and took private lessons. Learning the computer while recovering from a stroke is tough. If Mr. Golbus did it, it should be no trick for you.

Contact your local university or college for a list of computer courses and tutors. You can also contact the American Association of Individual Investors in Chicago and join its computer trading group once you get started. There is plenty of software that exists for today's trader. You should be sure that you and your broker have similar programs. And be sure you have a modem.

Tip 36

Eurodollars May Be the Place to Start

The biggest pit at the Chicago Mercantile Exchange is the Eurodollar pit. Yet the average first-time trader thinks there is more action in the S&Ps. Fine. First prove you can trade the Eurodollars and then we can do S&Ps. Or before you can fly the Space Shuttle, please take off and land a Piper Cub.

For those who believe you cannot make money with Eurodollars, I suggest you read the March 1995 issue of *Stocks and Commodities* magazine. "Commodity Trading Advisor" shows how a simple trend-following system made consistent profits in the Eurodollar. The author, George Panagakis, mentions four tips that may be useful to the off-the-floor trader:

1. *A simple trend-following system is superior to buying dips and selling rallies.*

2. *Don't use a related market to figure out what your market should do.*

3. *One indicator does not work in all markets. Different market indicators should be used.*

4. *A system can have more losing traders than winners ... just get rid of them quicker.*

Tip 37

What Do Traders Read Week after Week?

Simple. These are the newsletters and newspapers kept behind the counter at the Chicago Board of Trade and the Chicago Mercantile Exchange. Special thanks goes to Denise Love Walker, library technical assistant at the Chicago Mercantile Exchange, for her assistance. The following are the most popular because you leave a driver's license as security deposit: *Barron's, Grant's Interest Rate Observer, Cycles, Dow Theory Newsletter, Knight Ridder Commodity Perspective* (chart service), *The Economist, Elliott Wave Theorist, Commodity Traders Consumer Report* (for book reviews only; it is not connected with any consumer group), *Technical Analysis of Stocks and Commodities* magazine, *Spread Scope, New York Times* business section, *Financial Times*.

Private letters that have a following include: The Coz Report, Synergy Fax, Formula Research, Gann-Elliot Cycle Report, The Free Market Letter, Linnco Research Reports, Hightower Reports, Inter-Day Dynamics, Peregrine Letter, Optima, Moore Research Report, KCBT Market Watch (Kansas City Board of Trade), periodic letters from Midas Capital Management by Mark Boucher, and Dennis Gartman's Currency Letter.

Best no nonsense book, *Winner Take All* by William R. Gallacher, (Chicago: Probus, 1993).

Tip 38

Tactics Are Better Than Technical

What precipitates the current penchant for traders poring over indicators and ignoring tactics? Since most technical indicators are based on moving averages, the exercise is redundant. Really, how many indicators does a trader require? Three are enough. Ask the same trader to explore option or spread tactics and you get a firm "no" or "tactics are too complicated."

Soon our hopeful trader bounces from the indicator *de jour* to the indicator of the week and then to cycles. On the way, there may be a stab at overbought or oversold signals. But by then it is too late. You will run out of money before "gurus run out of indicators." Most traders know that markets take four steps up and two steps back on the way to moving higher. And while the technical indicators are being recalibrated and adjusted for market variation, the trader acts like a "blind dog in a meat house," being so close and yet frustrated from the real filet of a successful trade. The best traders are good tacticians, not technical historians. Traders understand this and don't get tricked into spending time looking for new indicators that are redundant.

Tony Donninger and Robert Morijn, who run the European Options Center in Moenchengladbach, Germany, recently visited the Chicago Mercantile Exchange for the expressed purpose of incorporating more tactics into their trading. "You can always find an indicator that will substantiate or defend your position while you are losing. The trick is to find a tactic that does the same thing without losing."

Currently, the European Options Center uses Call Ratio Spreads and Calendar Spreads to implement strategies.

Tip 39

Capitalism for the Middle Class, Socialism for the Rich

Deliberate and carefully designed press releases for swaying public opinion are propaganda. Remember the feature stories about free trade with Mexico and the countless economic benefits to our economy?

Didn't our government know the truth? A myriad of documents, including sources from the Mexican government and CIA, confirm that senior government officials knew the Mexican government and economy were in trouble before the free trade blitz started. Yet, politicians pressed for an agreement and got it. Then the bottom fell out of the peso and the Mexican economy.

The American people got hit with a $12 billion bill. We had protected the rich speculators who invested in high-paying Mexican bonds. Try to get that same deal for the middle-class American and you hear the argument, "Government can't guarantee investments."

Traders take economic news (nongovernment statistics) with a healthy dose of skepticism. The next time you hear the cacophony of government leaders supporting a treaty, an economic program, or defending a currency, take the other side of the trade. The best way to spot such a program is listening for the phrase, "Not only will this be good for your children, but also your children's children."

Tip 40

Healthy Leads to Wealthy

Although traders spend thousands of hours developing a day-to-day routine they hope will become profitable, they rely more on the high-tech tools. such as computers, and forget the athletes' Rule No. 1: Stay Healthy.

Traders realize that alcohol, caffeine, nicotine, and prescription drugs can affect trading performance. Before you dive into the psychological aspects of trading and blame your poor trading on lack of discipline, develop some type of exercise program. Most emotional decisions are made when traders lack sleep. They tend to make irrational trading decisions that endanger a good trading plan. If eating the richest, most fattening food is your way of celebrating a good trading day; your next trading day will be a disaster.

Can you get through a trading day without four cups of coffee? Can your broker?

Any seminar that offers cocktails, pizza, or promotes chemical-laden foods does not know the importance of nutrition and trading. At our seminars, we try to encourage a visit to the East Bank Health Club in Chicago. In fact, part of our seminars are held there. Look at the best and most successful traders in the business. Most look healthy. There are many wellness firms that deal with nutrition. You may wish to contact 24 Carrot Services, Inc., a wellness company in Madison, Wisconsin. Marc Levy is the owner and computer trader.

Tip 41

The Matter of Setting Goals

In September of 1988, Susan Arenson and I wrote an article for *Stocks and Commodities* magazine. After years of trading and giving seminars, the same ideas are still valid. Basically we stated:

> *In any area of pursuit, setting goals can give you a greater sense of direction, help you feel more productive, better mobilize your efforts, and direct your attention to the task at hand. When you set trading goals, you not only reinforce your persistence in developing trading skills but you decrease your trading anxiety, because you are focusing on learning to become a more disciplined trader.*

Tip 42

EEK!

This is not a scream. Rather, it is the badge for a CBOT member with 40 years of trading experience. During a recent member seminar, EEK stated two points that account for his reputation:

1. It is never too early to take a loss. Or you can never take a loss too soon.
2. A bad trade can ruin your day . . . and can ruin your week, your career, and your life.

It seems so simple and obvious. While the public is focused on creating a fortune, the professional trader is concerned with managing and taking a loss. EEK has been around for over 40 years. The average public trader is gone within 14 months.

There is no shame in being wrong. It's staying wrong that gets you into trouble. The market exacts a high price for hubris.

The Church Mouse, Wolverine, Sneaky Pete, The Gann Man (John Sievers), and other traders who trade with me also agree with EEK.

Tip 43

You Deserve a Break Today!

Sausage, bologna, franks, salami, hamburgers—if you consume them, why not trade 'em? As a trading commodity, the meat complex is less sensitive to international situations and market shocks.

Food service or the hotel restaurant institutional sector accounts for 50 percent of the beef tonnage to consumers. Since it is expensive to alter menus, the food service industry has a desire for price stability. Trading the meats may not have the international flair of Swiss francs, but trading the edible franks will allow you to miss the vagaries and vicissitudes of volatile markets.

Tip 44

The Ultimate Tip and It May Be Cruel

This will not come from the floor or the exchanges. It will emerge from the newfangled types of debt instruments and be carried to the market by financial wizards who appear in the financial press. A few already have arrived. They are on the talk shows and rave about a new era of economic life. They were teenagers during the 1987 crash and know only the buy side of the equation.

As individuals and institutions get seduced by the satisfaction of accumulating wealth, they will forget the basic law of economics: You cannot get something for nothing. John Kenneth Galbraith said it best:

There is nothing in economic life so willfully misunderstood as the great speculative episode. When a mood of excitement pervades a market or surrounds an investment prospect, when there is a claim of unique opportunity based on special foresight, all sensible people should circle the wagons; it is time for caution.

Today, banks are in the manufacturing business instead of the lending business. They trade their own creations and wander further away from their main business of lending. With commodity funds and large speculators, a financial wake-up call can turn into a financial panic within hours. We live in an anarchic global economy where trillions of dollars of stateless capital slosh around, beyond the control of most government officials.

As you watch new contracts being presented that have no real economic value, and a myriad of mutual funds hawked by new brokers, remind yourself that the next correction will be more than that. It will be more than a tip; it will be economic reality.

Place your stop loss now. As a rising tide can carry all boats, a sinking ship can take all passengers down with her. Locate and start wearing your financial life preserver. In a global economy the mood of investors can change with the click of a computer mouse. That mood is starting to change.

Tip 45

Breakout Systems Worked Great from 1980–1991

So purchasing a "breakout system," or testing one with data from the 1980s, is not relevant in the current trading environment.

Special thanks to John Strawa for that little gem, and floor trader "Bird Brain."

Tip 46

Traders Abhor Buying a Monday Morning Gap Opening

Think twice before chasing a market. Go the opposite way. Need help on gap openings? Call Don, "the Big Cat" at 312-902-6605.

Tip 47

A Mini-Course in Options

Options offer investors the opportunity to profit from price movements in the commodity markets. The options purchaser has the peace of mind of a known limited risk with unlimited profit potential.

Options make it possible to realize potentially substantial profits—often over a short period of time—with a relatively modest investment—and a predetermined limited risk. When options are purchased, the maximum risk is what is paid for the option, the option premium, and of course the transaction cost. When purchasing options you avoid the investors' nightmare of margin call—*being called upon on short notice to add additional funds to maintain your position or face a forced liquidation.* Options investors who purchase exchange traded options have the benefit of a limited risk and unlimited profit potential. In my opinion, this is why options trading continues to experience explosive growth as more and more investors become familiar with the advantages of investing in options.

There are two kinds of options. There are PUT options and CALL options. If you are expecting lower prices, you can make money as the market falls buying put options. If you are expecting higher prices, you would buy call options, making money as the market goes up. Since we are looking for higher prices in soybeans, corn, and coffee we would buy call options.

An easy definition of a call option is the right to buy something at a certain price within a set period of time.

And as the options investor you have the right to any increase in value above your purchase price.

So in general, as the market goes up, so does the value of your option. For example, if the price of soybeans goes up and the option increases by 50 cents, that would be a potential profit of $2,500 per option, or $25,000 on 10 options.

Soybeans & Corn

[1 Contract = 5,000 bushels]

[1 penny = $50.00]

And since options are liquid, they can be bought and sold at any time.

As for the downside, it's important to remember that you cannot lose more than you've invested. Obviously, if the price went lower, so would the value of your option, but options have *"Staying Power," the ability to withstand temporary dips in the market without incurring additional costs or risks*. In other words, if the market moves against you, you can hold on to your option and wait for an eventual turnaround. And if in the time remaining the market goes back up above your purchase price, you could be right back in a profitable position.

So in review, when purchasing options, the investor has a *predetermined limited risk, complete liquidity,* and the benefit of *"Staying Power."*

Tip 48

Your Broker is Like a Trading Co-pilot

So be sure to ask:

- Where do you get your research?
- How much experience do you have in the business?
- Give me three names of clients who would say you are a good broker?
- Have you ever been fined? For what?
- What real benefit can you offer me that my present broker cannot?
- Are you involved in other ventures besides brokerage? Why?
- Do the owners of your firm trade? Why not?
- Is your firm in the position you are suggesting to me?
- What is the last book you read about the markets?
- Do you have a night desk?
- What is your procedure for contacting me for margin calls?
- Is your net worth anywhere near mine? If not, how can you relate to my needs?
- What type of computer do you use?
- **What good are cheap, low commissions if I make losing trades?**

Part 3

Traps

Time Out for Perspective

Have you ever played tennis? When you understand the game and are confident about hitting the ball over the net, you begin concentrating on technique. There are various shots from top spins to slices. In other sports, like baseball, pitchers facing a batter have a myriad of pitches from change of pace to fiery fast balls. It's apparent that just getting the ball over the plate is only half the story. The following illustrates the point.

The once-Boston Braves wound up spring training one year by playing a game in Boston against the Red Sox. Warren Spahn faced Ted Williams once and struck him out with a letter-high fast ball over the outside corner. Afterward, Williams and Spahn chatted and Ted remarked, as they parted, "By the way, that fast ball you got me on was a great pitch."

Several years later, Spahn faced Williams again, this time in a clutch situation with men on base, late in the All Star game. Warren did not consciously remember Williams' earlier comments, but Warren's subconscious knew just which pitch to throw, and he threw it. As Williams trotted around the bases after he belted the game-winning home run, he was grinning at Spahn; puzzled at first, the light bulb lit up, and Warren yelled, "You son-of-a-bitch, you set me up!" Williams laughingly acknowledged it.

Harvey J. Blumenthal, *Tulsa Oklahoman (The Writing Habit: Essays* by David Huddle, published by Peregrine Smith, 1991.)

Just about every game has certain techniques. Some are psychological, some are folklore. Knowing when to use them and under what conditions is usually the first step in becoming a champion. Trading is the same. There are certain techniques traders use, depending on market conditions. The correct one can result in a home run. There are also traps.

With the explosion of software systems, many off-the-floor traders have relegated trading techniques to the category of slippage. Buying at the market, selling on the close seems to be the order of the day. Yet when you ask them about execution and money management techniques, they do admit they make a difference in profitability.

My research has revealed the concepts and techniques you develop on the floor are well worth the price of the seat. Incorporating these "tools" into your technical trading can only assist you in refining your trading skills. Besides having the advantage of location, time, and low commission, the floor employs "guerrilla tactics" that have been around for years. Avoiding these traps can only make you a more nimble and savvy trader.

Please Look Before You Leap— or Watch for Traps

When you see ads promising 50 to 300 percent return on your money, ask yourself why money managers who are struggling to just get 20 percent a year do not buy these systems and save themselves months and months of torment. Think about it. Money managers with millions of dollars under management could buy a system for $2,500 and eliminate the time and expense of computer programmers, research technicians, and support staff.

So why isn't this being done? Maybe because these great and wonderful systems are meant for the unsuspecting public.

Sorry, there are no secrets, except in Washington.

Seminars are useful, but do not believe the hype. I know many of these so-called gurus. Trading skills cannot be acquired within three days by sitting in a hotel room and taking a 20-minute tour of the floor. C'mon, would you trust your money to anyone who promised the secrets of trading within three days? Seminars and meetings are a good way to meet other traders and exchange ideas. But promoting secrets, citing "the Holy Grail" and so-called TRUTH as well as claiming to put you on "Easy Street" by touting scalping techniques as a track record, should be viewed with trepidation. This type of hype is more likely to engender regulation of the Futures industry than encourage trading. No one can teach you to trade. But you can learn to manage money. How much time do gurus spend on money management?

Usually not more than 10 minutes. The instructors that understand money and trading are worth seeking out.

As you browse through these traps, my comments may seem ingenuous. Or that I am attempting to cast aspersions on the trade. This is not the case. There are too many books on trading that always seem to stay on the periphery, so all you get is a limpid view of the market. I have stayed away from a plethoric style so you can get to the heart of trading. I have tried to avoid polemics and sententious banal maxims.

A great system will not make anyone a great trader. But a poor system in the hands of a good trader will still work. As Tim Slatter of Telerate stated:

The odds of being born with natural trading skills are slim. Most successful traders I know didn't start out with them. They learned winning skills through practice, practice, and more practice. The most difficult part of becoming a successful trader is not being blinded by trading's two seductresses: reckless greed and the sickening panic of fear. My advice is to "trade with your eyes open." People off the floor are called speculators. Why? The professionals in the trading pits are referred to as traders. Do you want to be a trader or speculator? Buy a seat if you want to be a trader, develop a trading plan if you want to be a successful speculator.

Those who know others are intelligent.

Those who know themselves have insight.

Those who master others have force.

Those who master themselves have strength.

Those who know what is enough are wealthy.

Those who persevere have direction.

Over the past few years, some of my former students claimed they knew my techniques and started charging students hefty prices to learn my approach to trading. While I certainly was flattered, it by no means had my blessing. So to avoid further chaos in the marketplace, I thought it was best if I presented these traps before more self-styled seminar leaders confused the public. As one trader who attended a seminar stated: *"Why talk to the monkey, when you can speak to the organ grinder?"*

Now, while I don't especially like being compared to an organ grinder, I'd rather not be the monkey.

Before you attend my day trading or computer seminars in Chicago, there are certain pitfalls you must avoid.

Typical Day Trader Traps

A long list, to be sure. But be sure you know them and guard *against* them!

- Wait for a good healthy trend to develop, usually a year.
- Get upset that you missed the move.
- Trade against the trend.
- When it goes against you, double up.
- Convince yourself you are right and the market is wrong.
- Go out and buy a trading system and do not bother to understand the basis of its trading suggestions.

- Be sure the system is high priced and claims unbelievable profits.
- Remind all your friends about how much money you are going to make with your new system. Do not remind your wife . . . she will remind you.
- Have unrealistic expectations . . . doubling your money every two months will do.
- Purchase a computer and take all the countertrend signals.
- Take a quick "Get Rich" course that promises to teach all you ever need to know about trading in three fun-filled days. Lunch is always included.
- Take the advice from radio shows sponsored by an out of town brokerage firm. Or buy courses from direct marketers.
- Be sure your broker is the age of your youngest son. And give him advice on why you are successful.
- Trade a market you know nothing about and succumb to high pressure salespeople who claim trading is the only way to be "above average."
- Be sure you have no idea of the market trend on a short-term or long-term basis.
- Take losing trades home overnight and pray that they go your way in the morning.

Day Trader Means Have a Different Attitude toward Money

We all have feelings and attitudes toward money—spending it, saving it, risking it—and the items that can happen to it—losing it or increasing it. In general, we also know that our total wealth cannot be increased a great deal or rapidly without taking some risk. If we work only for a salary and put some savings in a safe account, we will never expand our total wealth very much. Even buying a home carries some risk.

Telesis Management, Inc., a registered Commodity Trading Advisor, has a philosophy based on risk management. Since December of 1989, when the advisors implemented their current trading approach, they have a net gain of over 80 percent and a peak to trough drawdown of 2.38 percent. Certainly, the performance speaks for itself. Now, do you think they trade every day? Actually, they trade between 30 and 40 times a year. Yes, they do hold positions for more than one day. In the final analysis, you must determine what type of trader you wish to be.

However, a good day trade can be developed into an overnight trade and become a star performer. A Day Trade can be protected with options or a spread. Before you trade, know your "utility."

Utility measures how much something is worth to us: not price, or social value, or its "intrinsic" worth, but its worth to us personally.

The most important principle of utility—decreasing marginal utility—is again a matter we all have an intuitive grasp of (a mouthful, yes, but it is an idea we recognize in these examples):

> A $1,000 salary increase means a lot more to someone who earns $20,000 than it does to someone who earns $200,000.
>
> The justification for a graduated tax structure rests on the presumption that a tax payment of $250 pains the person who earns $10,000 more than one of $5,000 pains the person earning $200,000, even though the tax rate is the same 2.5 percent in both cases.

These examples reflect one aspect of the principle of decreasing marginal utility: The greater a person's total wealth, the less a given added (i.e., marginal amount) means to him or her. Further, even a constant proportional marginal increase has decreasing value as the amount of base wealth moves beyond the ordinary.

Another way to express this is to say, that as a person's base wealth increases, it takes an increasing proportional marginal increase to create a constant level of satisfaction.

To view this principle from another perspective, read through the next examples. Assume each trader has $100,000 base capital committed to trading.

> Trader Lifestyle Larry regularly takes $5,000 positions, sleeps well, and enjoys his weekends, even Sunday evenings.
>
> Trader Neurotic Nick takes similar positions, is always tired, and can enjoy a weekend only after a week of successful trading.
>
> Trader Risky Robert places large positions of her capital with equanimity.
>
> And, Trader Ivan the Terrible has trouble making decisions about $1,000 positions.

These examples illustrate a second important principle about utility: Each person has his or her own personal utility function, which means that even people with the same total wealth will respond differently to equal marginal or added gains (or losses).

A utility function questionnaire for trading would be a list of trading alternatives, involving differing degrees of money laid out, degrees of risk, amounts of gain or loss at different levels of payoff, and other questions. Using such a test, a useful utility function could be worked out for an experienced trader. He or she would learn something about each's feelings and attitudes toward risk, money, gain and loss, and other matters related to trading by going through the exercise.

The importance of a utility test is what it tells you, the trader, about your attitude toward trading and risk-taking with your money, your children's college funds, the money you set aside for your Caribbean cruise, or whatever. You can get a feel for these matters when you begin trading by thinking in ways suggested by the next few examples:

> If you begin a trading program and find you cannot get to sleep on Sunday nights, cut back the amounts risked on Fridays to a level that permits you to sleep well.

If you feel comfortable with the amounts you ordinarily commit to trades and you have won some and lost some, consider raising the proportion of capital at risk. Make sure that the fraction risked, however, is not so large that a run of bad trades would put you close to ruin.

In a recent book called *Trading Tactics of the Pros,* the following misguided statement appeared:

The market does not give you or deny you money—it is something which you give or deny yourself. How much we reward ourselves is directly proportionate to how deserving we feel we are. . . . The same is true in trading. No matter how solid or successful an approach to the market is, a trader is only going to "allow" himself as much money as he feels he is entitled to—regardless of his conscious intentions.

Obviously, this is a blatant dumb sales pitch and completely ignores the concept of Utility.

Now let's go on to the Traps!

Trap 1

10 to 30 Percent Pull Back—Please Calculate

A 10 percent pull back in a position seems quite normal. But remember, a 10 percent pull back in Soybeans selling for $8 is 80 cents. A stock selling for $65 will experience a $6.50 loss at 10 percent. Traders look especially to buy at 10 percent pull backs when the stock and or futures contract is receiving publicity or experiencing a trading range. Unless you are convinced this is the last time in your existence you will have the opportunity to catch a move, you usually will receive a 10 percent pull back to enter. If you are currently in a position, prepare for the pull back. It will happen. The pull back may extend to 30 percent and even as much as 62 percent.

Most markets "run and pause" and then backtrack. That is how you get stopped out. Traders will usually scale in their buying to take advantage of these bargain days. At the start of any move you generally experience a pull back of 38 percent, 50 percent, or 62 percent. These pull backs occur quite frequently and are measured from the start of the move to the most recent high. The further pull backs are usually most indicative of a stronger move, with the current trend.

Trap 1: *10 to 30 Percent Pull Back—Please Calculate* 137

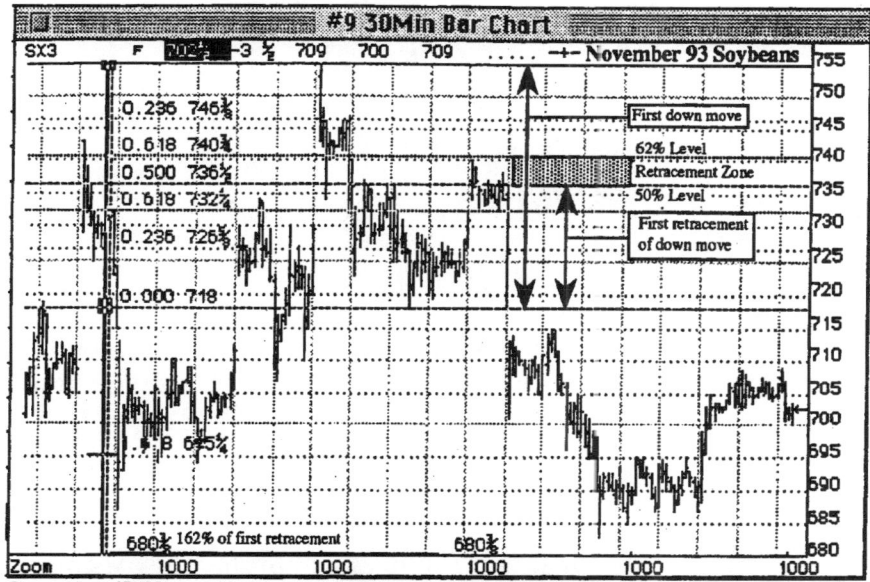

Example of Trading Trap #1

Trap 2

Convincing Yourself that There's Big Bucks in Futures

A good friend of mine on the floor researches all the commodity markets, keeps charts by hand, and hardly ever trades the Futures markets. Let me run that by you again: Hardly ever trades. He has such contempt for the "games" played in the industry, he will only trade options when there is fundamental news that the floor cannot manipulate. Sound cynical?

My friend owns a beautiful home in a suburb, takes vacations regularly, and invites me over to swim in his outdoor pool and view his greenhouse. His home overlooks Lake Michigan, and it is really scenic in the summer, especially with the private beach.

Why does he keep in touch with the futures market? Because he is a trader, not necessarily a Futures trader. He will use the information related to the commodities industry to trade other markets. If Gold looks like it is going up, he will buy Gold Stocks. If Bonds are going up and interest rates are going down, he will buy stocks that pay high dividends. Silver going up? Why not buy the actual metal?

That is my point. You can use the information generated by the commodities market and trade other markets. Think of yourself as a trader, not merely a Futures trader. My friend does not want to leverage 10 percent on a contract that is going to expire. It is easy to get Futures myopia. Cross over and decide how you can use some of the ideas generated in the Futures market for creating alternatives. When you trade the market, remind yourself there is more than one market. Constantly ask yourself: How can I create this same trading opportunity in another investment vehicle? By doing that you develop the mind-set of a trader.

Trap 3

Hold On—but Know When to Buy

Public Relations Ploys: Companies send signals to shareholders about the direction of their company. Trading on this news can be counterproductive and is usually in the market.

Television Story: If negative, stay out. Consider buying after correction runs its course. If positive, wait until market stays open and see if there is any follow-through.

News Story: If negative, and reportedly by a noted columnist, you could be in trouble. Story reported by the public relations department usually has no effect.

Equity Sales: Negative effect on prices.

Stock Split: Usually prior to announcement. Buy the news, sell fact is a good strategy.

Trap 4

IPOs Take the Money and Run

It is easy to be attracted by tantalizing stories of overnight profits in new stock offerings. But you should know that institutional investors tend to get the choice issues before the public. According to the American Association of Individual Investors, the small investor does not get the best piece of an initial public offering.

If you do get on the ground floor of a good opportunity, bail out within 90 days.

Roni Mechaely, an assistant finance professor at Cornell University, studied over 900 initial stock offerings from 1984 through 1988 and found an average 8.5 percent gain on the first trading day. Some investors succeed in getting new issues with a tactic of opening several accounts with major brokerage houses. The best tactic: If a broker calls you out of the blue with an initial stock offering, run the other way.

The real top-line issues do not require a full-blown publicity campaign. The typical cycle of a new stock is crucial to learn. About six weeks after an initial public offer, the stock gets a booster shot based on research from the underwriters. The price tends to erode as the insiders take over. Underwriters usually allow corporate officials to sell three to six months after the offering. **For this reason alone, your trading tactic is to avoid holding a new issue for more than three months.**

Trap 5

Running Stops... Will Generate False Indicators

There is a bit of fiction surrounding the floor trader's ability at running "stop" orders placed by the public. Actually, the stops are usually run by large speculative houses, places where you may place your own trades.

Local traders get caught the same way. It is not uncommon for large traders to hit the bids of local traders and then force them to cover. The scenario goes something like this:

What's the bid? (Done by large speculative house.)

60 bid, fine sell you 10, What's the bid?

55 bid, fine sell you 20, What's the bid?

50 bid, fine sell you 30, What's the bid?

45 bid, fine sell you 75, What's the bid?

40 bid, fine sell you 50, What's the bid?

The pit is quiet or maybe there is a weak 35 bid. The locals have been buying, and at every turn the market is being forced lower.

Now the trader who has been selling becomes the bid. "45 bid," the trader yells. Then, "50 bid."

What do you think happened to all the traders who sold the market at 45 and 40? They are running over each other to get out of the trade. Meanwhile, at your computer screen, you think there is a sell signal and you may even get caught in the downdraft noise. You call your broker, and then it is too late. You were faked out.

It is very difficult to protect yourself from this type of tactic. Option traders and Spread traders are not concerned about this type of ploy. That is why having some type of Option protection for your position will help you ride out these roller coaster moves. In some cases posting more than 10 percent margin is usually necessary so you don't get mowed down by this trap.

Trap 6

Political Turmoil, Don't Bet Patriotic

When a country is experiencing political turmoil, sell its currency. Either buy Puts or sell Futures. Or sell the weak currency and buy a stronger one. On July 17, 1992, the Nikkei lost 121 points to settle at 19,805. This type of dramatic move is a signal to sell the Japanese currency. By June 18, 1993, the Japanese yen was down 158 points at the CME at 9:30 A.M. By the end of the Merc's trading day the yen was down 228 points. Even holding the position over the weekend resulted in another 100 points.

On June 21, 1993, the yen closed down.

This was not inside information.

How can you get this information? Many news services are available via modem. Or you have the ability to call the night desk of your trading firm. Or maybe read the *New York Times*. Yes, it is that easy. On page A4 of the *Times*, James Sterngold filed a story on June 17 with the following headline: *"Battle over Japanese Politics May Force an Early Election."*

This story was in the papers hours before the CME opened. The lead paragraph just about told traders what to do.

A Threat of Paralyzing the Government

The long-running fight here over cleaning up the scandal-plagued electoral system led to open political warfare today, increasing speculation that Prime Minister Kiichi Miyazawa may be forced to dissolve Parliament and call an early election. The battle threatens to leave the Government paralyzed during a meeting of the Group of Seven major industrialized countries here in three weeks.

Trap 7

Attention Day Traders: Gann Is Not Elvis

(If you have never heard of Gann, skip this section.)

We have a saying, "You are never far from a Gann Line. Or you will run out of money before the gurus run out of cycles." The favorite game in seminar circles is to find one or two examples where numbers may have worked and build a system around them. This type of "factitious" argument is not really believed by professional traders. What is sad is the fact that this opprobrious behavior makes novice traders feel obtuse. Here is an example from a recent newsletter:

> The stock market crash in October was 5.5 years from the first day of S&P Futures trading in April 1982. This month is 5.5 years since the October 1987 crash. There may be some symmetry around the 19th of April. *What the heck does this mean?*

Traders use abridged Gann numbers for a trading reference. With so many people using it you may want to keep the following concepts in mind. Identify the high-low range over the life of a particular commodity and then identify key support and resistance levels within this range. Gann used relationships based on multiples of $\frac{1}{8}$ and $\frac{1}{3}$.

The method of calculation is straightforward. Start by subtracting the contract low from the contract high to produce a range. I may also do this for a yearly high to low configuration. This range is then multiplied by these constants: $\frac{1}{8}$, $\frac{1}{4}$, $\frac{1}{3}$, $\frac{3}{8}$, $\frac{1}{2}$, $\frac{5}{8}$, $\frac{2}{3}$, $\frac{3}{4}$, and $\frac{7}{8}$. Consider a commodity with a life of contract low of 100 and a high of 340. To produce levels, the following computations are used:

1. Subtract the low from the high, 340 − 100 = 240.
2. Multiply the range by a series of constants:
   240 × ⅛ = 30
   240 × ¼ = 60
   240 × ⅓ = 80
   240 × ⅜ = 90
   240 × ½ = 120
   240 × ⅝ = 150
   240 × ⅔ = 160
   240 × ¾ = 180
   240 × ⅞ = 210

The resulting values set up the following levels:

Low, ⅛, ¼, ⅓, ⅜, ½, ⅝, ⅔, ¾, ⅞, High
100, 130, 160, 180, 190, 220, 250, 260, 280, 310, 340

The amount of importance as well as time and effort you wish to place on Gann analysis is up to you. However, Mr. Gann never sold the rights to his name; his son never went into the business. There are many people professing to be Gann traders. The best advice: If you use Gann to get you into a trade be sure you have enough money for Gann to get you out of it. But don't worry, you are never far from a Gann line and that may be the best money management system ever. Get out at the next line.

Trap 8

"Goofy" Trading . . . or Falling in Love with Your Position

Part of my job at such prestigious firms as Disney and Warner was encouraging stock purchasing. In the marketing business, huge sums of money are spent trying to get the public to buy. Disney offers stockholders a 10 percent discount on theme park products plus colorful stock certificates with pictures of the Disney characters. People will actually hang onto the stock because they "love Mickey." Well, I like Mickey, too, but it is a little goofy to hang onto a stock because you like the characters. Once buyers are committed to a position, their ego reinforces the positions. Traders will stay in a bad position longer than a bad marriage.

While on the staff of the Chicago Board of Trade, I was told the purpose of the Futures market was risk transfer and price discovery. However, for the concept of risk transfer to succeed, interest must be created by market makers or commercials at the time to effect risk transfer. If you haven't guessed, the Futures market has to seduce the maximum number of traders to the wrong side at important decision points. If this cannot be accomplished, risk transfer would not work. There would not be significant people on the other side or wrong side of the market. Ever wonder why some technical indicators do not always work? Because technicals do not move the market, psychology does.

One reason is that the chart patterns encourage you to BUY so the commercials can SELL. After all, higher prices lead to more buyers and, if you are a seller, you are apt to get a better price. If you want to sell a product, you want the highest possible price. The people who will pay these prices are folks who are uninformed and do not know the real value of the commodity. That unfortunately is the public. They look at charts and not the true cost of the goods and services. The next time the newspapers are screaming about certain stocks or commodities "going to the moon," ask yourself who would be foolish to sell at these prices. Usually, it is the owner of the product or stock. And our friend Goofy may be buying.

Trap 9

Press the Market and You May Be Taken to the Cleaners

This is a trap to avoid during the last hour of the trading day and especially going into the close of the market.

Pressing is adding to an existing position in the hope the market will make new lows on the close or new highs. The public tends to forget that the floor accounts for 50 percent or more of the volume. The average trader may sell late in the day, while the floor is buying. Since most floor traders do not care to go home with a position, you can get caught in a rally going the opposite of your position. Also, be aware that the Mid America stays open anywhere from a few minutes to over an hour after the Chicago Futures Exchange closes. If there is a strong trend, it will have follow-through at this Exchange. For those who use closing prices in their analysis, the Close of the Mid America may be a more accurate number. Floor traders will tend to press the market when prices are falling, especially if the public is long and a new low can be made. However, you are not a floor trader and lack the response time.

A falling market will move three times as fast in one-third of the time as a rising market. Let the floor press the market; you want to be out of your trade before the close of the trading day. If you are placing Market on Close orders too often, you are not trading smart.

TRADER'S DISCUSSION In the immortal phrase:
  WOULD'VE, COULD'VE, SHOULD'VE . . .
  OR HINDSIGHT IS ALWAYS 20/20.

If you had purchased lumber, you could've made a fortune; but you didn't, so now you can't. This type of quixotic logic is rampant at brokerage firms and in the trader's mind. It is also used by people trying to impress you with a track record that shows one great obscure trade in the Egg pit that made the entire year. The "Would've tactic" is used against the unsuspecting public and makes them blind to the reality of trading.

Trap 10

When Traders Go BONKERS

Grant Noble, who lives in Lake Forest, Illinois, told me about this and it seems to be true from a psychological standpoint.

When a trader loses more than 20 percent of her money to the market, she behaves in an irrational manner. A trader's tactics and style of trading will erode to the point of taking ridiculous "shots" in a vain attempt to recapture money lost.

When you lose 20 percent of your equity you must retreat, regroup, and revise your trading tactics.

Trap 11

Trading in a Vacuum

Be sure your home or office price screen resembles the price boards of the exchange that you trade. This is key to viewing the market the same way as the floor. Having Bonds and Coffee on the same screen does not make sense. Besides the lead contract, your screen should also display the back months. Typically, a move will start in a back month and Spreads will more than likely signal a move in the market.

Most newsletters are written so you receive the information on the weekend. Eager traders act on Monday buying or selling, depending on the recommendation of the newsletter. Try to contain your enthusiasm—chances are the market will come back to the price in the newsletter. Use the first few hours of trading on Monday to let the market settle down. Seems counter-intuitive. Tuesday is the day for getting down to business. That may hold true for other industries. As a trader, the position you make on Monday may haunt you for an entire week. Wait a few hours before trading.

Trap 12

Act in Haste, Repent at Leisure

Before you trade a new market, wait at least two days. Use the two days to chart the market. Consider a trade on the third day only if you are convinced the risk/reward ratio is worth entering a market you have never traded before. The waiting avoids the so-called no-brainer trades that traders are prone to take based on rumor. Make your trade early in the day so, if you are wrong, you have the rest of the day to get out. Never enter a new position in a new market on a Friday and carry it over the weekend. With international trading, you can get in on a Sunday night and still make the trade. Waiting two days will allow you to get some fundamental information from the exchanges or the "opinion leaders."

Recently, a technician told an associate to buy Oats because the chart looked good. But two days of research revealed the following:

- The Oat pit at the Chicago Board of Trade has one broker and just a few traders.
- Since 1982, we are importing Oats from other countries and that will offset domestic demand.
- Experts say we now produce 300 million bushels of Oats, down from 1.5 billion in 1955.
- The American Oats Association cannot improve Oats' competitive edge.
- Farmers are not interested in planting Oats because of low prices.
- Imports are keeping prices down. Oats are being imported from Scandinavia and Canada.

- Beyond human consumption, demand has been decreasing for decades. As animal feed, Oats are projected to be 225 million bushels, less than half the total of a decade ago.

With these facts, my friend took another look at the great Oat trade and took a pass.

Trap 13

Raiders of the "Lost Motion"

Jim Hyerczk, who teaches Gann theory at the Chicago Mercantile Exchange and coteaches at our Day Trade seminars, concentrates on this phenomenon in the marketplace. According to Jim:

Market reactions are not changes in trend, many fall under Gann's label of Lost Motion. This happens when there are slight breaks through chart patterns by market momentum. As a trader, these fake-out moves can trigger stops and then turn around and have the market rally against you. Most of these "lost motions" are found in penetrations of tops, bottoms, 50 percent retracement areas, and geometric angles. If you are placing your stops around these areas, you will more than likely get hit.

In an ideal world, you should place your stops where there is a trend change. But as Jim reminds us, it is easy to get faked out. As a market moves higher, the change of trend areas are wider apart. Place your money management stops and change of trend stop around the same area. If you find that you do not have the money to accommodate both criteria . . . maybe you should trade another market. "Lost motion" really leads to lost money.

Trap 14

Systems Self-Destruct, Will Your Trading?

No matter how great your system is, no matter what kind of track record it generates, it has the seeds of its own destruction.

Here's why. A coin flipped an infinite number of times will have a ratio of 1:1. Equal heads and tails. But every 1,000 flips or so, heads or tails will show up 10 times in a row. Every trading system lives with that possibility. That's why you must control the profit/loss ratio of your system. When markets are trending, it seems like profits never end (but remember you are maintaining a high profit to loss ratio); when they are within trading ranges, most systems begin their course to self-destruction. Altering your trading system may be in order—or be prepared for meltdown. You can be snared by the laws of probability.

Trap 15

Let's Just Watch It . . . Don't Kid Yourself

You are in a losing trade. You are near your stop loss. You cancel your stop loss and practice self-deception by muttering, "Let's just watch it." Maybe you give this instruction to your broker. In short, you have a mental stop. The next time you utter "Let's just watch it"—you had better watch out. There is a steamroller coming your way and your name is engraved on the front roller in red letters.

Trap 16

The Traders Trap . . . Sinking in Quicksand

The English translation of this Latin phrase, "The world wants to be deceived. Let it, therefore, be deceived," goes back a thousand years.

The biggest self-deception is referring to yourself as a trader when you have another full-time job. You cannot be a trader and a dentist. There is a Pit Goddess and she will not allow it. She is the only person in the world who will grant the title "Trader" and she will not grant it to part-timers. But you can be a dentist and a speculator. You can be in a managed account. But you may not be a trader. That is perhaps the biggest trick the public makes. Believing they are traders while the real traders take their money.

When your broker calls and suggests a trade, substitute the word *speculation* and you won't be upset when you lose. All your commodity trades take place in a pit. The pit traders are locals. They make their money by getting yours. They buy below value and sell above value for an instant in time. Are you on par with them? This does not mean you cannot make money speculating. If you start perceiving yourself as a speculator, you will accept your position in the commodity "food chain." Don't be flattered by a broker telling you that you are a trader. Traders do not have brokers. They make their own decisions. As a speculator you must **have a longer time horizon** and follow your system and money management approach with rigor. Intuition and feelings have no place off the floor. Your computer can't pick up the emotion of the pit. But you can succeed. Stop worrying about each tick. After all, most floor traders hope to be off-the-floor traders, too.

Trap 17

Buy with Pride, Hold with Confidence (The Grizzly Trap)

When the market is going against the public, speculators can get stubborn. Pit traders are hoping the public that bought with pride will hold with confidence. The last days of a move down changes the market from a bear into a giant grizzly bear. Traders like to sell no lows, the public likes to hold. Buy the first break.

Go ahead, buy the second break.

You will be the third break.

Trap 18

Today's Market Wizard Can Be Broke Tomorrow

There is no doubt that you must build intellectual capital before you can build personal wealth. So, if you are going to read biographies, concentrate on traders who made fortunes, lost them, and made them back again . . . and left a legacy.

One such trader is Bernard Baruch. His advice and counsel were sought by four Presidents, and his investing and trading strategies are substantiated by an incredible legacy left to his family. No, he did not give courses or trade by the stars and moon, but his advice stands firm today:

1. Don't try to buy at the bottom and sell at the top. This can't be done—except by liars.
2. Learn how to take your losses quickly and cleanly. Don't expect to be right all the time. If you make a mistake, cut your losses.

One inning does not make a ball game, and reading biographies of traders who had two or three good years and then "blew out" may be entertaining but certainly not much more. Look for biographies of consistent traders and not those in the incipient stage of their career. And for gosh sake, stay away from anyone who claims they can predict the market, and give you discipline.

Trap 19

Futures Education ... I'm So Broke, I Can't Pay Attention

The scenario usually starts: You make a little money trading. You start reading the trade magazines. If only you could "jump start" your trading. But how? And then. Pow! You see it. Seminars, tapes, hotlines—all wrapped around the guise of Futures education. Who are these people? Where do they come from? They must be good or they wouldn't advertise, right? Wrong! The amount of unregulated commodity educators claiming they teach trading and promising you winning trades is nothing short of awesome. Not even gambling schools in Las Vegas resort to this type of bodacious "snake oil" advertising. Little wonder 80 percent of the public is on the losing end. Yet few public traders test the credibility of these schools. Would you attend a school where 80 percent of the graduates were unsuccessful in their chosen careers?

"The combination of technology, optimism, and the success of some highly visible traders can easily lead to unrealistic expectations," says Perry Kaufman in his book, *Smarter Trading*. Recently a Florida-based chart service stated: "Without any previous training, education or experience ... I will tell you how you can use these same powerful-profit strategies to enjoy amazing profits." The ad copy continues, "It's not uncommon for my subscribers to double, triple, or even quadruple their money."

What are they actually selling? It's a paper chart that's mailed after the market closes on Friday so people can receive it by Tuesday. In all fairness, they do manage to locate a few people who made money trading. It's much like lottery advertising. Find five people out of 900,000 and promote the heck out of them.

Pat Arbor, the current president of the Chicago Board of Trade, stated in *The Outer Game of Trading* (Chicago: Probus, 1994), "And yet the public, to a large extent, hasn't gotten that message. They think it's all about purchasing the Delta Signal or Master Trader Software or some delusional system that doesn't have a chance of working."

Nelson F. Freeburg, who publishes *Formula Research*, can quantify how well-advertised systems work. He recently tested 22 popular trading systems. He comments:

> *For those seeking the Holy Grail, I can report that few offered consistent profits across the universe of commodity markets. Some methods for trading the British pound were not nearly as profitable with the D-mark—still less with crude oil—never mind the S&P 500. Even when the focus was a single market, returns were often uneven when the scope of testing was broadened to span a market's entire price history.*
>
> *Even when a system does work, you need extraordinary patience and an incredible money management system.*

The real trick is distinguishing education from entertainment. As a former advertising copywriter and an executive associated with such enterprises as MTV, the Walt Disney Company, and the Movie Channel, I can understand the ways in which promotions are construed for fact. Most of your direct mail solicitation is expensive entertainment. But how do you know?

Your first clue is the instructor's lack of association with an exchange or university and the fact he or she has an advertising and public relations firm working with a large database. The reputation is created by publicity and direct mail, not by any academic or trading standards. Sometimes the instructor will claim "Trade with Our Money"—but alas, it is really your money, since he or she simply raises the price of the seminar to accommodate margin requirements and any loss.

The second clue becomes apparent when you discover the class fee is two and three times greater than exchange or university courses. Or, when the course is sponsored by a trade magazine that does not pay the speakers, but rather promises them a forum for their school or products. Selling the names of students so direct mail promoters can market more useless information is not the sign of a company concerned about your education. There is no way a magazine should be promoting seminars, because this compromises its editorial integrity. Did you ever notice that magazine-sponsored seminars are tied in with the biggest advertisers?

The third clue is the use of words like "secret" or "dream team of gurus" and color brochures with shots of scintillating smiles on perfectly coiffured heads. The real secret is, **there are no secrets.**

If you are still in doubt, inquire if your instructor is a registered Commodity Trading Advisor and then ask for samples of articles, books, or studies. Also ascertain if your instructor is a broker or has an affiliation with any salespeople at the seminar. In short, are you paying for a sales hustle or education? Finally, ask for any monthly commodity or securities statement with his or her name on it. Does the instructor really trade? Or is it paper trading? Does he or she trade using a computer? What type? What kind of program? Ask for a copy of the trading plan.

One can only teach trading by example. Students must be involved in the thinking and doing process. Standing up and giving pedagogical examples or reading notes from exchange-developed material does not do it.

And even if you read a thousand books and attend all the seminars, there is no substitute for real trading. Perhaps a historical perspective may further the point. In the book *Counterattack* (New York: Putnam, 1994), the author W. E. B. Griffin takes the reader into the cockpit of a Wildcat as fictional pilot Charley circles the carrier *Saratoga* in December of 1941.

> *There was a crank on the right side of the cockpit. It had to be turned no less than 29 times to release or retract the gear. The mechanical advantage was not great, and to turn it at all, the pilot had to take his right hand from the stick and fly with his left hand while he cranked hard, 29 times, with his right hand. . . . Charley had learned that, if he*

unlocked the landing gear, then put the Wildcat in a sharp turn, the landing gear would attempt to continue in the direction it had been going. Phrased simply, when he put the Wildcat in a sharp turn, the landing-gear crank would spin madly of its own volition, and when it was finished spinning the gear would be down.

The main character, Charley, would not have known about the landing-gear trick from reading a book. He knew about this "trick" or insight from piloting the Wildcat. And so it is with trading: You must trade.

The successful floor trader takes advantage of watching, seeing, and participating in hundreds of trades in the pit. Usually, there is a mentor or trader group to join during the trading day. A bank trader is part of a group where a senior trader guides and directs the new trader. The off-the-floor trader has no model for behavior. Most of his or her knowledge is cognitive. It's like learning brain surgery by reading a book. There are people claiming to offer guidance to the off-the-floor trader. But alas, it may be a broker who is more concerned with generating commissions than seeing you succeed. It reminds one of the character Mephistopheles.

Verify the credibility of the teacher who promises the "scoop" on trading. Call the National Futures Association and check if your teacher is a Commodity Trading Advisor. Ask about complaints. Inquire about credentials. Does he or she teach for a recognized exchange or university?

Registration does not in any way guarantee the honesty of a firm or individual. Nor does it imply the person or firm is recommended by the NFA, CFTC, or any other government agency. The ultimate decision to register for a course rests with you. According to the CFTC, your best defense against "being fleeced" is a prove-it-to-me attitude. Get all representations in writing and be skeptical of promises. A 30-day money "ironclad guarantee of satisfaction" that systems promoters preach is required by any firm using the U.S. Postal Service.

Now this may seem like a lot of work. But it won't cost you more than a few phone calls. After all, some people will investigate the purchase of a car more carefully than a commodity education. And yet down the road, the wrong education and ensuing bad trade will cost you more than the automobile.

Russ Wasendorf and Thomas McCafferty in their book, *All About Options* (Chicago: Probus 1993), elaborate on promotion concepts:

> *Promotion that delivers an unbalanced presentation of the enormous profits to be made from the market with little or no mention . . . is in violation of federal regulations. Second, beware of whoever is presenting the materials. If their initial overture is so out of tune, the rest of their song will probably be as well. So the question on every trader's lips, "Where do we go from here?"*

That's easy. While everyone is marching down the yellow brick road to Oz, you take the following steps.

The following is a list of courses taught at the Chicago Mercantile Exchange. Your core knowledge should be built around those with asterisks.

Japanese Candlestick Analysis Technical Analysis.

Managed Money (taught by Patricia Gillman, Esq.).

Currency Trading.*

Fundamental Analysis.*

Interest Rate Hedging.

Introduction to Futures.

Introduction to Gann Theory.

Introduction to Market Profile.

Managed Futures.

Money Markets and Futures Pricing.

Pit Trading.

Point and Figure Insights and Application.*

Spread Trading.

Stock Index Markets.

Technical Analysis.*

Trading Technologies.*

Wycoff Volume–Price Analysis.

Series #3 Course** (before you sign up for any course, obtain the study materials from the Futures Industry Association in Washington, D.C.).

Once you are familiar with these concepts, ask your software vendor or date vendor for the names of traders in your immediate area. The off-the-floor trader must have a basic knowledge of computers and how to access information. Vista Trading and Research provides solid background for the users of Trade Station. Other computer vendors do the same.

In my opinion, the best Futures program is a two-week program taught by the Chicago Mercantile Exchange in August. Contact the exchange for a brochure on the program. If you stay at home and trade with a computer, you will not learn much hanging around a commodity pit with a local for two or three days. Why not ask your commodity broker for the names of people who are successful and who trade the same way you do? Speakers who speak for free are really salespeople. Avoid them. The second-best courses are offered by Vista Trading and Research, and American Association of Individual Investors.

If possible, pay all courses with a credit card so you have 30 days to change your mind and get a refund. Or suggest to these "peddlers of futures knowledge" that you will pay them a high percentage of the incredible wealth they will shower upon you.

Trap 20

Getting Stuck in Charts

The following trap from Bob Bouson of Foremost Futures argues a great case for pausing before sinking into the quicksand of chart formations: Without volume, open interest, and fundamental knowledge, chart patterns can give you a sense of euphoria. Bob is in the class of broker/trader and is a frequent speaker at our seminars.

> *I was perplexed and without a guide. Everywhere traders knew about triangles, wedges, head and shoulders, tops and bottoms, and the rest of the classical chart formation theory—thanks to Edwards and Magee—yet everywhere traders were losing money. The theory itself, it seemed, could not be without merit. After all, a small group of traders and the publisher of a widely read futures newsletter preeminent among them have at least until now used classical chart formation theory successfully. Why was it, I mused, if the theory were sound, as I had to think it was, and known by traders, that people were not making money with it?*
>
> *I had two clues, which led me to suspect that the difficulty lay in the application of the theory, rather than in the theory itself. When I went back to look over anthologized historical charts covering times during which I had been actually trading in those markets, I clearly saw important and successful formations, which, to my dismay, I had not seen in those same markets at the time they appeared.*
>
> *My second clue was the result of extraordinary good luck.*
>
> *I discovered a remarkably reliable indicator. The indicator works this way: When a price chart can be read as being ambiguous—that is, presenting either bullish or bearish formation, depending on how one interprets it—and, in the face of this ambiguity, the brokers were unanimous in seeing only the bullish formation or seeing only*

the bearish formation, the formation that the crowd of brokers did not see was the most likely to be successful.

I have come to call these "invisible" formations, because they are unseen by so many traders. I have suspected that its origins lie in the human inclination to see within ambiguous and disorganized data what we have prior expectations of seeing.

Trap 21

No News: No Clue for Day Traders

In the famous book *The Art of War* (New York: Delacorte, 1983), Sun Tzu states, "We are not fit to lead an army on the march unless we are familiar with the face of the country—its mountains and forests, its pitfalls and precipices, its marshes and swamps."

If you are not familiar with a market and the reports, you will be going into battle risking complete financial annihilation.

Patrick Robinson, who runs a special services desk at Peregrine Financial, is more direct: "When I field calls from the public asking what just happened that made the market move, I refer them to the trading calendar."

Trap 22

Don't Confuse a Good Trader with a Bull Market

Or maybe the old phrase "a rising tide carries all boats" is more appropriate.

The trend is up and that is obvious to anybody who can read a chart. Even my 14-year-old friend David Poll from Main Man Enterprises tells me that. "Neal, it's easy to be right when everything points that way."

And because the guru of the month is riding the bull market is no reason that you tag along. When everybody sees the Bull Market, the real trader is ready for the other side of the trade. In his book *Crisis Investing for the Rest of the '90s* (New York: Carol Pub. Group, 1993), Douglas Casey states:

> *Exceptional managers and management philosophies exist, but the average fund buyer mistakes a bull market for genius. Few of the more than 3,100 funds are managed by geniuses. There is no reason to place much confidence in the managers of most of today's thousands of funds. Most of them were not in school during the last bear market and few of them have seen anything but a bull market.*

There is something unsettling about having inexperienced cadets managing huge portfolios. Even hiring the best and the brightest does not always work. Fidelity Investments, the country's most powerful mutual fund, used this approach and still failed in its bond fund work. The penchant of taking big bets with the hope of making home runs works in a bull stock market but not in bonds. Traders know that a bullish bias can make you excel at trading one type of instrument and be your downfall in another.

Trap 23

My Broker, My Son

Retaining a broker the same age as your son or daughter may pander to your parenting ego, but eventually will not be profitable in the long term. Most young brokers are fresh out of school and barely have money in a savings account. Besides, many don't trade.

Would you give your own son or daughter $25,000 to speculate? Would you take the kid's advice on financial matters? What is so special about brokers who are about the same age as your kids? They usually are good at getting money out of their parents . . . that's because they are persistent.

Floor traders do not have brokers; we have clerks and we do not take their advice. There is one exception—do they have money on the trade they are suggesting?

Trap 24

Tendencies Are Not Realities

The following graphs show tendencies in various markets. Keep these so-called seasonals in mind, but also know they can be traps if followed blindly.

It is easy to construct a so-called seasonal chart. All that is needed is historical data. Seasonals should be no more than 30 percent of your trading decision. I saw a good friend of mine lose his wife, house, and savings accounts blindly following a seasonal that was 95 percent accurate.

The German trading group, Impact Investments, in Duesseldorf, said, "You can never predict human nature and it is not seasonal." Nevertheless, "We keep it in mind when we trade." Usually in the "back of our minds."

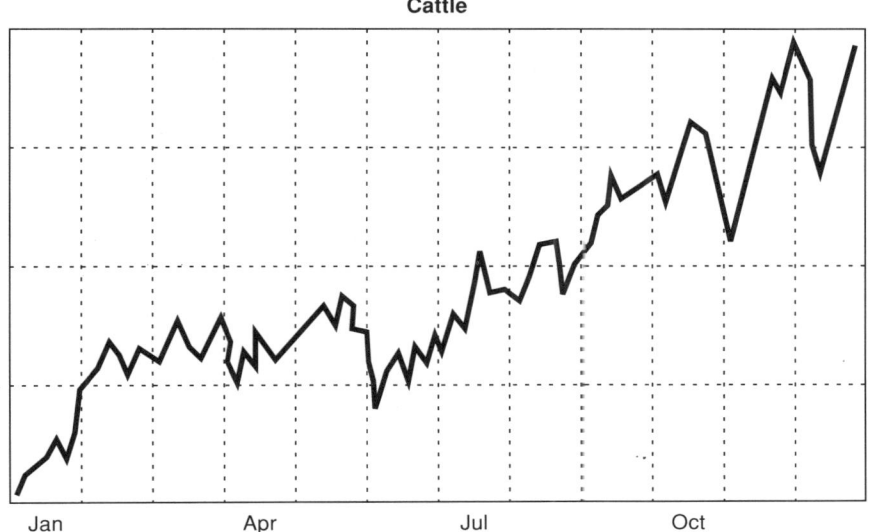

By Hal's Chart Service

172   Part 3: *Traps*

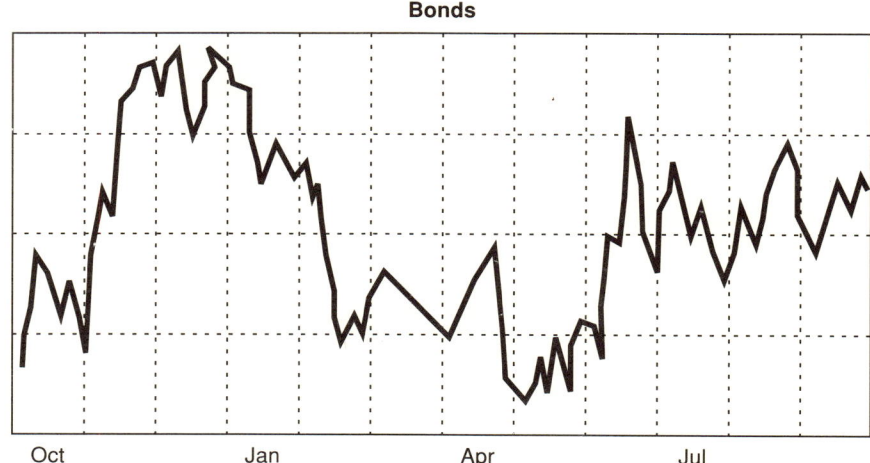

Bonds

Oct   Jan   Apr   Jul

**Remember seasonals can be traps. Use them as guides only!
By Hal's Chart Service**

Part 4

Spreads

Since Spreads could be classified as Tricks, Tips, or Traps—depending on the use—I decided to give them their own section. However, it is also an opportunity to "sit in" on my class, Spread Trading at the Chicago Mercantile Exchange.

Spread 1

May Corn/March Corn

FUNDAMENTAL The primary corn crop harvest occurs in October. Once the grain is stored, carrying charges should widen in the subsequent months, since supplies are abundant. Full carry on this particular spread is approximately 14 cents. As the March contract approaches delivery, winter transportation difficulties, combined with seasonal increases in demand, may produce a bullish environment. It is advisable, therefore, to exit the position before first notice day on the March contract.

TIP   Initiate: **First week in January**

Close: **Last week in February**

TECHNICAL Given its trading range characteristics, it is advisable to enter this spread on weakness and place a mental stop only beyond the lower boundary of the range. Conservative traders may take partial profits on breakouts above the upper channel line of the range.

HISTORICAL During the preceding four years this spread confirmed its trading range behavior with a bias toward a carrying charge market. As shown most prominently, once the position begins to move down toward the end of February it should be exited promptly. Because this movement tends to indicate bullish pressure in the market, aggressive traders may wish to consider reversing position at that time and establishing a long March/short May spread. When doing so, care must be exercised due to the possibility of delivery in the nearby contract.

Spread 2

December Corn/July Corn

FUNDAMENTAL Referred to as an "old crop/new crop" spread because it includes the December contract, the first futures month of the new crop. When the trade is initiated, uncertainty over acreage yield and demand typically translates into either a substantial premium to the July side or a narrow premium to December. As this uncertainty resolves, there is less upside pressure on the nearby contract, and the spread begins to favor the deferred. Full carry is approximately 48 cents. Since anything near this level is unlikely until later in the year, a profit objective of 8 to 10 cents is reasonable.

TIP **Initiate: Third week in January**

Close: First week in March

TECHNICAL The old crop/new crop nature of this spread suggests that it should behave in a trading manner. Trendlines are useful directional indicators and appear to be more reliable with this spread than overbought/sold measures. Movement in this spread beginning in January often traces out an Elliott Wave pattern of either five waves up or three waves down. If the January high is exceeded by the middle of February, this is a strong signal that the position should continue favorably until at least sometime in March.

HISTORICAL In years in which the spread is profitable, it tends to present a buying opportunity on a retractment occurring near the end of January. The longer the market takes to regain upside momentum, the less likely the spread appears to move favorably. For traders who consider taking only partial profits in March and holding the balance of their position until later in the year, highs that occurred near the end of February typically represent subsequent resistance.

Spread 3

September Corn/ July Corn

FUNDAMENTAL This spread involves two contract months within the same crop year. It is designed to capture the seasonal widening in carrying charges, which occurs following harvest and before the July contract month enters delivery. Full carry on the position is 13 cents. In a strongly bullish market, the nearby contract may gain on the deferred and the spread would then react unfavorably. For this reason it is important to monitor price action in the lead month for signs of strength in the market.

TIP   Initiate: Second week in February

        Close: First week in March

TECHNICAL Volatility in this spread begins to increase as the July contract becomes the lead month. Until then the position tends to trade within a range of approximately 28 days between successive highs and lows. This cyclical behavior can be used to more precisely time the entry and exit, as can overbought/sold indicators with time periods equal to one-half the cycle length. Trend measures should be avoided with this spread, because of the high probability of whipsaw. Mental stops should be placed outside the trading range formed since the beginning of the year. Rather than trying to identify a bottom in the spread, a position should be established during February after the deferred month begins to gain on the nearby month. Once a position is initiated it should be added to only on pull backs that do not break below the lower channel area.

TRICK This spread has tended to stay within a five–eight cent range in the February–March period during the last several years. While this presents limited potential gain, it also indicates less risk in carrying the position. Some traders may prefer to take advantage of reduced margin requirements for grain spreads and increase the total number of positions they are carrying. Even in years in which the overall spread has moved unfavorably, a bounce up in March sufficient to exit with little or no loss generally develops.

Spread 4

September Soybeans/ May Soybeans

FUNDAMENTAL Due to the processed products of soybean meal and oil, soybeans are affected by supply/demand considerations for both feed-grain and oilseeds. Since the bean crop year begins September 1, this is considered an old crop/new crop spread. Uncertainty over the new crop helps support the price of the deferred contract, and during the first two months of even bull years, the May contract tends to lag the lend months. It is, therefore, only in strongly bullish years that this position should behave unfavorably. Full carry is 92 cents.

TIP Initiate: First week in January

Close: Last week in February

TECHNICAL This position tends to experience a sharp down move late in December, following which is the optimal time to enter the spread. Once opened, the position should be tracked using trend-following techniques. The dominant direction for the spread is indicated by a series of higher highs when it is trending higher or a series of lower lows if it is heading lower. Each major wave approximates the 21-day short-term cycle for soybeans. Overbought/sold measures and channel formations are not particularly reliable, because of the trending characteristics of this spread. Additional positions can be added on pull backs, provided the overall trend continues favorably. Mental stops should be placed below the most recent low and adjusted only once a higher low is made.

TRICK In years in which the spread has been profitable, it has managed to hold the low set near the end of December. When this low has been broken, the position has tended to move lower. The

move higher: A possible double top formation occurring in December is also a signal of potential adverse movement. Highs made near the middle of February are often met with weakness immediately thereafter, so partial profits should be taken on strength during that time. If the immediately preceding low is penetrated, then the remaining positions should be liquidated even if before the targeted date of exit.

High Risk Spreads 5 and 6

Spread 5

Buy February Hogs/ Sell April Hogs

TIP Initiate: First week in August

Close: 200 points February Hogs over April Hogs

TRICK The tendency of February Hogs to gain on April Hogs is well known in the Hog pit. April is usually a weak month for this Spread. February can be strong when there are weather-related problems in the Midwest.

It is best to place the Spread when February is 40 to 80 points over April. Do not risk more than 110 points on the Spread.

TRAP High Risk

High Risk Spread

Spread 6

Buy Wheat/Sell Corn

TIP **Initiate: Before September crop report**

Close: Day after crop report

This spread should be done using the December contract. The objective is to take advantage of a large Corn crop. If you decide to keep this Spread on, exit the first day it goes against you. Please consult the *Wheat/Corn Spread* booklet from the Chicago Board of Trade. It is available at no charge.

TRAP High Risk

Spread 7

March Soybean Meal/ July Soybean Meal

FUNDAMENTAL Soybean meal is processed either as a light protein feed ingredient or is further refined for direct human consumption. Demand for meal tends to be relatively strong during the beginning of the year, and, since meal does not store well, current demand is satisfied primarily with nearby supplies. At the same time, requirements for deferred delivery are less certain. Brazilian soybeans are not harvested until March, so they do not contribute to supply early in the year. Exports and projections of domestic consumption are important factors to watch for signs of demand that will impact the nearby contract.

TIP Initiate: **First week in January**

Close: **Middle of February**

TRICK This spread works better in predominantly bull markets, in which demand for soybean products should produce an upward trending configuration. Weakness in the chart late in December should produce a near-term low early in January, and this is the signal. Frequently this break will bottom near the September–October low, and this is a good area to begin considering the position. Confirmation is given once the spread begins to move higher. After the position becomes profitable, it should not be carried below the point of initial entry. Because of its possible volatile nature, the spread should be added to only by traders willing to assume higher risk. Partial profits can be taken near the end of January, and no position should be carried past the recommended closing date.

Spread 8

October Soybean Meal/ August Soybean Meal

FUNDAMENTAL This spread is designed to work even without a substantial change in the underlying cash price for soybean meal. The carrying charge between these two deferred months should widen progressively into the year as storage charges between the delivery months account for a greater percentage of total storage. In addition, the supply of soybeans, which becomes available as a result of the Brazilian harvest in March, should produce less demand for the nearby contract. These relationships will invert only during periods of extremely strong demand or of diminished exports from Latin America.

TIP Initiate: Third week in February

Close: Middle of May

TRICK Ideally, this spread should move within a narrow range with an upside bias from February to May. The time of entry can be refined using overbought/sold indicators to measure the break, which typically begins early in February. One statistic to pay particular attention to is the Crush Margin Spread, which relates soybeans to their primary products, meal and oil. The crush ratio is constructed around meal production, so a rising crush indicates increased demand for meal. This could translate into an unfavorable movement in the October–August spread. The crush margin is calculated by multiplying the price per ton of meal by 0.024, the price per pound of oil by 0.11, and subtracting from the sum of these the price of soybeans per bushel. Since the crush spread is used here as an indication of changes in demand for meal, the relationship should be tracked over time when drawing conclusions.

Spread 9

July Soybean Oil/ March Soybean Oil

FUNDAMENTAL Increased supply of soybean oil as a source of the fall harvest is the primary driving factor behind this spread. The crush level increases in the fall, which leads to expanded oil supplies and tends to widen carrying charges. It is important to exit the position before the results of the Brazilian soybean harvest in March, for a reduction in output there can produce a sharp increase in demand for domestic products. Weekly exports and monthly stocks should be monitored for possible changes in supply, which could impact the spread, also.

TIP Initiate: Middle of December

Close: Last week in February

TRICK Entry in this spread follows a cyclical downturn, which typically occurs during the first two weeks of December. Overbought/sold indicators as well as support from the October–November lows can be used to refine the exact entry. Once a position is entered, the spread tends to oscillate with an upside bias, so additional contracts should be added only on pull backs. A breakout above the December high is a valid indicator of further strength; and, if such a penetration occurs, the position should be exited on weakness pulling the market back below that level. If the December high cannot be broken, this signals possible weakness and opportunities to break even or take small profits should be examined. Soybean oil follows a short-term cycle of 21 days, and this spread can be expected to track this interval. Indicators should be constructed using a period equal to one-half the cycle length.

HISTORICAL It is important to open this position following a break in December, because a second entry opportunity is seldom presented. In recent years this break has been followed quickly by a sharp rise, and this should be used to take at least partial profits.

High Risk

Spread 10

May Soybeans/ May CBOT Wheat

FUNDAMENTAL Soybean harvest occurs in September and October, while wheat is harvested in late May through July. At the beginning of the year, the bean supply, therefore, is known, while the size of the wheat harvest remains uncertain. As the year unfolds, estimations of the wheat crop become more accurate when the supply of harvest grain nears. In addition, the relatively higher price per harvest for soybeans tends to widen the carrying charge differential in the two commodities. All these factors combine to ordinarily increase the price of beans relative to wheat.

TIP Initiate: **Middle of February**

   Close: **First week in April**

TRICK This spread is best studied using trend-following techniques. After a period of relative stability during the previous three to four months, the spread often experiences a drop beginning late in February. Completion of this break is the signal to enter a position. From there trendlines can begin to be drawn, and even simple moving averages will assist in confirming a change in trend. Although additional positions can be added, they are best done on pull backs that do not break support lines. Wheat has a short-term cycle of approximately 32 days, and this spread will often oscillate within a period half that long. A penetration of the February highs is a strong signal that the position will at least meet the profit objective. Once it does, partial profits should be taken. If the position begins to back up from there, the remainder of the contracts should be exited even if less than one month after initiation.

TRAP Traders wishing to carry their position into April should observe the sharp downturn that typically occurs later in the month. Although there are times when the spread then reverses and continues its climb, carrying the position after this break entails greater risk.

High Risk

Spread 11

November Soybeans/ December CBOT Wheat

FUNDAMENTAL This new crop spread is designed for differences in harvest periods between soybeans and wheat harvest when the supply of a grain is set. Further supply will not emerge. Before harvest the expectation of adjustments is likely to depress prices. On the other hand, soybean tends to be strongest into the new year just as wheat begins to decline. This combination suggests that beans gain in price relative to wheat.

TIP Initiate: **Third week of February**

Close: **Within the first to third week of June**

TRICK The spread operates with a slight upside bias from March to April or May. Corrections during this period tend to be brief and do not reach into new territory. Because of the narrow range, it is difficult to apply other technical indicators than long-term trendlines to measure support and resistance. Oscillators will prove inherently late in signaling changes in direction. The frequency of reversal makes this a spread to take small profits when they arise and not wait for a major move. On the other hand, once initial profits are taken, the position may be reentered on subsequent weakness with the same profit objective. It may be helpful to follow the May–March Soybean spread for signs of strength in the lead months.

HISTORICAL For traders wishing to hold the spread longer, volatility does not seem to increase until well into April or May. Even then the bias continues to favor the carrying charge position, although still within a narrowly defined range.

Moderate Risk

Spread 12

July Soybeans/July CBOT Wheat

FUNDAMENTAL The propensities for this spread are similar to those for the May Beans/May Wheat position. Because the July delivery follows the May, this spread is opened slightly later in the year and is held approximately one month longer. By carrying the position into the beginning of wheat harvest, it is more sensitive to changes in that commodity. During the summer, wheat will often gain on beans, because the wheat harvest is complete and the soybean harvest is approaching. For that reason the spread should not be carried into delivery.

TIP Initiate: Last week in February
Close: Third week in May

TRICK This position is best analyzed with trend-following methods. Long-term support and resistance lines can be drawn from extremes as far back as data are available. Chart formations, such as double and triple tops and bottoms, also are indications of probable price reversal. Overbought/sold measures can be used to time entry and exit, but period length should be chosen carefully to avoid premature signals. Once the initial position is established, additional contracts can be added on pull backs that do not violate previous lows. Partial profits should be taken whenever the spread reaches an overbought condition, since corrective breaks can be sometimes significant. Due to increased volatility into delivery, the entire position should in all cases be exited at least one month before the contracts go into delivery.

HISTORICAL In all but one of the past nine years this spread has exhibited weakness from October to February. This is due primarily to an increased supply of soybeans following harvest. As this supply becomes integrated into the market, the spread typically reverses its long-term direction and begins to advance.

Spread 13

Sell a Teenager

TRICK Sell Calls and Sell Puts with 19 or less days left to expiration. Hence, the work teenager. Most of the time premium or theta runs out in this period.

TIP **Be sure there are no government reports that might influence the market in a dramatic way.**

TRAP If you forget to place a stop loss it could mean disaster. Do not be talked into any type of bogus delta neutral position. A delta neutral position is like a dinosaur on your front lawn. It must always be fed.

DISCUSSION Best to use the OEX for this type of trade. The OEX was originated in 1983, and is a basket of blue chip stocks. In this type of spread trade you must consider: Market outlook, volatility, and strike prices.

For fine tuning this trade contact Tim Mouton at 1-800-880-4572, Ask for his OEX strategies on Teenagers.

Moderate Risk

Spread 14

June Live Cattle/ August Live Cattle

FUNDAMENTAL Cattle experience their greatest marketings in late fall when they come off grass and are placed on more expensive feed. Lows occurring at that time are followed by rising prices into late spring or early summer. This pattern favors the bull spreads in most years. The greatest risk to the position is large placements of cattle on feed early in winter, which will translate into increased beef production by spring. This would tend to depress prices in the nearby contract. When considering this spread it is important to monitor the monthly *USDA Cattle on Feed Report* for changes in herd size.

TIP Initiate: Third week in January

Close: Second week in April

TRAP Get out before cattle on feed report

High Risk

Spread 15

June Live Cattle/ October Live Cattle

FUNDAMENTAL This spread follows the seasonality of the cattle market during late winter. Typically, tight supplies and a strengthening cash market tend to support the nearby contract. Increases in spring placements of cattle on feed, compared to the winter, raise the expected supply for October, which depresses the price of the deferred contract. Large placements in winter, feedlot liquidations, and competition from pork and poultry products are the primary market risks.

TIP Initiate: First week in February

Close: 150 points or the first week in March

TRICK This spread moves in a trending manner over a regular cycle lasting approximately 10–14 days. This cycle can be used to time entry as well as to select exit points. Trendlines may be drawn from either the December or January lows, and positions should be exited upon a subsequent penetration. Other trend-following techniques should be avoided, because of their lag in signaling a directional change. Sharp rallies tend to be followed by equally precipitous declines, so it's preferable to exit a trade early, rather than wait until the spread begins to reverse. If January highs do not exceed those of the previous month, this suggests possible weakness and lower prices ahead. Mental stops must be placed far enough away to allow for intraday volatility, which in the cattle market sometimes can be substantial.

TRAP The decline that begins in January may extend beyond the first week in February, so timing the entry for this spread can be difficult.

Spread 16

June Live Hogs/ April Live Hogs

FUNDAMENTAL Seasonal patterns in the hog market are now less important than they once were, due to improved breeding and raising methods. Nevertheless, since corn is still the primary feed for hogs, as it rises in price the number of hogs sent to slaughter typically increases. This relationship ordinarily occurs from February through the beginning of April, and increased supplies tend to favor the bear spreads. Cash hog prices should be monitored, since an inverted market in which futures trade at a discount to cash indicates strong demand, and it is the type of environment in which this spread would not perform well.

TIP **Initiate: Middle of February**

Close: First week in April

TRICK When this position is opened, the deferred contract should be trading at a 200–300 point premium to the nearby month. Anything substantially greater than this suggests the market may already have adjusted for increased supply, and further upside potential is limited. Until the April contract goes into delivery, it is unlikely the spread will display large volatility, thus trend-following methods should be avoided. Hogs have a short-term cycle of approximately 21 days, so particular attention should be paid this long after the most recent high or low. Chart formations are notoriously unreliable in the hog and pork belly markets, so no particular significance is placed on pattern recognition. Mental stops should be placed outside the range of daily volatility and above the low of the last 30 days.

TRAP If the spread does not advance soon after it is opened, then additional positions should not be added on subsequent breaks, since the likelihood of a sideways pattern is increased. In only one of the last five years did the high price in March exceed that from February, highlighting the importance of selecting properly the point of initial entry.

High Risk

Spread 17

April Live Cattle / April Live Hogs

FUNDAMENTAL This spread is designed to profit from the different seasonal tendencies in these two livestock markets early in the year. Cattle prices generally gain as supplies diminish, and slaughter declines when grazing pastures become available in the spring. This assumes the usual light placements of cattle on feed in early winter. Pork supplies during this same period are usually plentiful and exert downward pressure on hog prices. The primary risk in the position is the possibility of large early winter placements, which could keep cattle prices from rising in the spring.

TIP **Initiate: First week in February**

Close: First week in March

TRICK When positions are initiated, the premium should be less than 25 cents per pound basis the cattle. Otherwise cattle prices would have to rise sharply before the spread becomes profitable. Sharp peaks make this position difficult to trade using trend-following techniques, although lines connecting previous tops or bottoms can be used to project overall direction. Additional contracts should not be added later in the month, and partial profits can be taken whenever the spread reaches an overbought condition.

Spread 18

April Live Cattle/ April Feeder Cattle

FUNDAMENTAL During late winter, feeder cattle prices typically reach their seasonal highs for the year. This is a spillover from the tendency of live cattle prices to increase from December through February. Strength in live cattle prices translates into higher feeder cattle prices during this time of year. The correlation is broken once supplies expand when winter feeders begin becoming available. This generally occurs around the time of delivery of the February Futures contracts. Because cattle are placed on feedlots an average of 5½ months before being sent to slaughter, this spread is more speculative than one with contracts spaced that far apart.

TIP **Initiate: First week in March**

Close: Last week in March

TRICK Since the April contract in both live and feeder cattle becomes the lead month at expiration of the February contract, this spread may exhibit extreme volatility surrounding that expiration. For that reason, no positions should be opened until the February contract expires. With a recommended holding period for the entire position of not more than one month, additional contracts should not be added on subsequent weakness. To measure intraday fluctuations, hourly charts on the spread should be kept if possible for several weeks before initiating a trade. If the position is logged on, the feeder cattle side should be opened first, because that is ordinarily the more difficult side to establish. Total open interest in feeder cattle futures is often less than 20 percent of that for live cattle. After a profit of 100–150 points has been achieved, at least a portion of the positions should be closed.

Spread 19

June Live Cattle/ May Feeder Cattle

FUNDAMENTAL This spread should normally reach its greatest extreme sometime in late January or early February. At this time supplies of feeder cattle are near their lower mark, while live cattle prices should not reach their seasonal peak until late March or early April, coinciding with the time recommended to close this position. Monthly *USDA Cattle on Feed Reports* as well as cash market prices should be studied for signs of supply shifts in these two related markets.

TIP Initiate: Middle of March

Close: Between the first and 10th of April

TRICK It is common for this spread to exhibit an Elliott Wave progression from the lows in January and February to the highs in April. Impulse waves within this sequence can be used to take partial profits, while corrective waves provide the opportunity to add new positions. Trendlines drawn from recent lows are reliable confirmations of the overall trend, and overbought/sold measures are useful in determining when each impulse wave is probably nearing completion. Short-term trading cycles do not appear clearly with this spread, and so selection of optimal periods when constructing various indicators is difficult. As an initial approximation, one-half the normal cattle cycle of 15 trading days can be tried and then refined based on correlation with past price action.

TRAP This spread has moved favorably, although to different degrees, in each of the last 10 years. Entry in March should occur following a correction from the advance above the lows made in February. A penetration through the downward sloping trendline from highs made the previous year confirms a change in long-term direction and increases the likelihood of higher prices in the spread. Aggressive traders may consider reversing their positions in April as the seasonal top in live cattle develops and the spread typically falls at least through the end of May.

Spread 20

August Live Cattle/ August Feeder Cattle

FUNDAMENTAL The seasonal pattern of this spread is less pronounced than with other live cattle/feeder cattle spreads, because price extremes reached during the first few months of the year have less of an effect on the deferred contracts. Nevertheless, this position tends to follow the nearby months as the supply of feeder cattle increases while live cattle prices continue to rise. The greatest risk is development of the bottleneck in cattle marketings, reducing the price of live cattle and causing the feeders to become overfed.

TIP Initiate: Middle of March

Close: 100 points or five weeks

TRICK Analysis of this spread is rendered more difficult by the fact that it has at times trended and in other years stayed within a narrow trading range. When the position has trended the highs in early March exceeded those of the preceding month, and in that case oscillators should be avoided in favor of trend-following techniques. In trading range years, additional contracts should not be added on breaks, because of the limited upside potential. In those years, interim profits should be taken on rallies, and indicators should be constructed using one-half the normal cattle cycle of 15 days. Traders wishing to follow the correlation between feeder cattle, live cattle, and feed grain may wish to track the so-called Cattle Feeding Margin spread. This relationship measures the difference between feeder cattle and corn on the one side and live cattle on the other. The ratio is usually 4 feeder cattle and 3 CBOT corn contracts (5,000 bushels each) to every 7 live cattle.

Spread 21

June Deutsche Mark/ June Swiss Franc

FUNDAMENTAL   A spread involving foreign currencies is sometimes referred to as a "cross." Movement in the position is a function of changes in relative value of exchange between the two markets, which in turn depends on the level of interest rates within the two countries. This spread frequently bottoms into the end of the year, presumably as traders reduce their market exposure during the U.S. holidays. After the first of the year, new positions are established with the Deutsche mark gaining on the Swiss franc for such reasons as demand for West German exports and reduced concern over "safe haven" investments.

TIP   Initiate: **Last week in January**

Close: **50 points or the first week in March**

TRICK   Given potential volatility in the cross, this position should be approached using trend-following techniques. Lines drawn from price extremes during the last quarter of the previous year provide useful levels of support and resistance, as do congestion areas occurring during the same period. Because of the potential volatility, additional positions should not be added later, while rallies that take the spread into overbought areas can be used for taking profits. Whenever trading Currency Futures, it is important to monitor the overnight EFP market for movements that occur outside the normal daily trading period.

Spread 22

December Treasury Bills / March Treasury Bills

FUNDAMENTAL As the maturity of a debt instrument increases, the interest rate associated with it typically increases to compensate lenders for the additional risk they assume. This relationship is shown graphically by the normally upward-sloping yield curve, which plots the rate of interest as a function of time. A flattening in this curve tends to be relatively brief and indicates greater demand for short-term funds, as is often the case near the end of the year. Once the curve begins to resume its normal shape, instruments of longer maturity gain on short-term instruments. This adjustment is captured in Treasury-bill futures by initiating a bull spread with contracts nine months apart.

TIP   **Initiate: Middle of December**

       Close: First week in March

TECHNICAL The yield curve typically covers a period from 90 days to 30 years. As such, the six-month duration is only a small portion. Prices for instruments of this maturity should gain gradually as the slope of the entire curve rises. This is reflected by a slight upward trend in the spread, culminating as the lead contract enters delivery. Because T-bill futures trade inversely to the rate of interest, as rates decline the price of the futures contracts will rise. The spread will most likely advance when the deferred contract is trading at a discount to the nearby during the end of the year. When a substantial premium to the deferred month already exists, it is less likely that further gains in the spread will develop. This is particularly true if the rate on overnight federal funds does not spike upward during the final trading days of the years.

HISTORICAL It is not uncommon for a slight downward correction to occur around the third week in February; and if this develops, the position should be closed then and not held until the lead contract enters delivery.

Lower Risk
Spread 23
May Orange Juice/July Orange Juice

FUNDAMENTAL The crop year for oranges runs from December 1 through November 30. Harvest in Florida begins in December and is typically completed by the middle of June. The supply of frozen concentrated orange juice, on which futures are traded, depends primarily on yield, which in turn is a function of weather conditions. Since maximum production can be calculated assuming ideal temperature and moisture, speculation centers on how far below this level actual production will fall. Late winter freezes will ordinarily have a bullish impact on the market and cause this spread to widen.

TIP **Initiate: Middle of January**

Close: Last week in March

TRICK After a prolonged period of sideways movement, this spread should begin to exhibit a slight upward bias near the first week in February. If it does, a support line connecting past lows can be drawn and positions should be maintained as long as this line is not broken on a closing basis. Although higher risk, additional contracts can be added on breaks that do not violate the long-term support line. December highs must be taken out before the position has a high probability of success. This should occur ideally sometime in February, although occasionally it has happened as late as March. Orange juice futures exhibit little or no cyclic content, so construction and application of overbought/sold indicators can be difficult.

TRAP Since the high price in March is frequently followed by a brief but sharp correction, it is better to take profits as the market enters an overbought condition, rather than waiting for it to reverse direction. There is little consistency after this reversal, so carrying positions later in the year is not advised.

Spread 24

July Cotton/ December Cotton

FUNDAMENTAL The cotton crop year in the United States runs from August 1 through July 31. Planting begins in March and harvest is generally completed during December. The July contract is the last of the old crop year and December is the first of the new crop year. This "old crop/new crop" spread, therefore, is subject to fluctuations between crop years. Full carry is approximately 390 points, and the spread is expected to reach nearest this level when demand is low and expectations for the harvest are high. This typically occurs during December or January. The *USDA Cotton Planting Intentions Report*, issued after the first of the year, should be monitored for the expected size of the new crop.

TIP   **Initiate: Last week in March**

         Close: Middle of June

TRAP The spread is subject to high volatility and should only be entered after indication of an upward turn in an oversold market. Indicators to measure this condition should use a period of approximately nine days, which is equal to one-half the length of the trading cycle for cotton. Due to the possibility of sharp reversals, additional positions should not be entered on breaks. If the chart has formed successively lower highs from November through January, a line connecting these represents resistance during the first months of the new year.

HISTORICAL It is not uncommon for the break, which often begins in March, to continue through the first week in April, and for that reason a position should be entered only once it appears the decline has ended. If the spread moves favorably, there will still be sufficient profit potential even if some of the upside has been missed.

High Risk
Spread 25
May Lumber/July Lumber

FUNDAMENTAL Lumber production is largely unaffected by seasonal considerations, since most mills can operate on nearly a continuous basis as warranted by demand and reflected by price. Volatility is primarily a function of consumption, which is indicated by such factors as interest rates and new housing starts. The bull side of this spread has behaved well historically, because demand for lumber increases with the usual expansion in new construction during warmer weather. In addition to domestic demand, signs of foreign consumption are also significant, since the United States continues to export plywood, lumber, and logs internationally.

TIP Initiate: First week in January

Close: Middle of March

TRAP Substantial volatility is possible with this position as the demand for lumber varies. The spread tends to move in one direction for more than a few days once it begins, and this phenomenon is true during both primary and corrective phases. Although lumber has a short-term trading cycle of approximately 19 days, oscillators and other overbought/sold indicators generally prove unreliable due to the large fluctuations that can occur. As a result of this volatility, profits should be taken when the spread still appears strong, since reversals of even one day can be substantial. It is preferable to enter positions only after the chart begins to move higher following a decline. Greatest strength occurs when the nearby month trades at a premium to the deferred, and the position should be initiated only if the two contracts are trading near or above even. Never fade a limit up move (i.e., this market).

Spread 26

The Platinum/Gold Spread Indicator for Bonds

It seems every trading day brings a government or private report that moves the price of bonds: retail sales, unemployment, consumer confidence, purchasing managers' index, etc. The reaction to these reports often generates meaningless churning that confuses fundamentalist and technician alike.

If the bond market is difficult to trade long term, the obvious temptation for the average futures trader is to trade bonds short term. But floor traders pay only about $1 every time they trade. An off-the-floor trader not only pays commission but also the difference between the asking price and the bid price (usually one tick in a liquid market like bonds or $31.25 a contract). If that off-the-floor trader attempts to day trade one contract every day, he runs into an opportunity cost of a (on average) $25 commission plus the $31.25 one tick bid/ask difference or $56.25 total. Over 240 trading days in a year, that's $13,500 total just to break even—and that doesn't include the cost of "real time quotes" and other expenses. That makes day trading a sucker's game for all but the most brilliant off-the-floor futures trader.

One way to generate longer-term bond trades is to use an old floor trader rule that my friend Grant Noble promotes. Just before the broadcast of a major report that affects the bonds, place a buy stop 16 ticks above the present price and sell stop 16 ticks below the present price. If the report triggers the buy stop, put a protective sell stop 8 ticks below your entry point. If the report triggers the sell stop, place a buy stop 8 ticks above your entry point. If neither stop is triggered, both expire at the end of the day and you wait for another report to place new stops. Once in the market, you use your protective stop until a "report stop" is lower than your original protective buy stop or higher than your original protective sell stop.

For example, let's say September bonds are trading at 100 just before the June unemployment report issued the first week in July. You place a buy stop at 100–16 and a sell stop at 99–16. A bullish report triggers your buy stop and you place a sell stop to protect your long bond contract at 100–08. The bond market continues to move higher. A week later, just before the June Producer Price Index release, the bond contract is at 103–16. Now you place another buy stop at 104 and a sell stop for *two* contracts at 103—one to liquidate your old long and one to go short. The sell stop for two contracts takes the place of your old protective sell stop at 100–08.

While Grant believes this old floor trader rule will make you money over the long run, even 16 ticks stops can get "whipsawed" in violent but trendless trading. In addition, sometimes after a report the bond market will move past your 16 tick stop and you will get filled far away from your stop order, eating into potential profits. In Grant's opinion, the best use of this floor trader system is to "pile on" a winning position you've already established before the report. There is an indicator that can help you anticipate the direction of bond reports that doesn't depend on your knowing some expert with a Ph.D. in economics—the Platinum/Gold Spread Bond Indicator.

The prices of all commodities have speculative and industrial components. Copper could be rising in price due to early industrial demand; or it could also be rising due to rampant speculation by commodity funds, the latest speculative fad among the public, and/or the type of buying panic copper consumers have at the end of a long price rise. If copper is rising in price due to long-term, sustainable industrial demand, that will show up in the coming months' economic data and depress bonds. But if copper is rising due to raw speculation, then now is the time to buy bonds depressed on "inflationary" copper prices and sell them when the coming months' industrial data shows weak demand that will rally bond prices.

Spread 26: The Platinum/Gold Spread Indicator for Bonds

Platinum has a much larger industrial demand component than gold. In the free-floating price era of old, a big discount in the Platinum/Gold spread (like 1982) is a sign of a severe recession which is usually followed by a big bond rally. A big premium (in percentage terms) of platinum over gold (like 1986–87) is a sign of large industrial demand and is usually followed by a low in bond prices (like October 1987).

While it is true investment fads can hit platinum and artificially lift its price against gold, this is far less likely than the "buy every metal in sight" mania that periodically hits the commodity funds and the public. Normally, a big rise of platinum against gold will show up in a few months' time as strong economic data that will hurt bonds and vice versa. Here are some examples over the last few years:

Platinum/Gold Peak	Bond Price Low	Platinum/Gold Low	Bond Price Peak
May 1991	Late June 1991	Late August 1991	October 1991
Early October 1991	Late October 1991	December 1991	January 1992
March 1992	April 1992	Late April 1992	May 1992
Early June 1992	Late June 1992	August 1992	Late September 1992
Late October 1992	November 1992	November 1992	December 1992
December 1992	January 1993	Early March 1993	Mid March 1993
April 1993	May 1993	Late June 1993	Early September 1993
Late August 1993	November 1993	Late November 1993	January 1994
Late March 1994	May 1994	Late May 1994	June 1994
August 1994	November 1994	December 1994	April 1995
Early May 1995	June 1995	Late June 1995	Mid August 1995
Fall 1995?	Winter 1995?		

Sometimes a turn in the platinum/gold spread is followed by an opposite reaction in the bonds in only a few weeks. Sometimes it takes several months before the signal shows up. Like any trading tool, it has to be used with other indicators and not as some infallible "Holy Grail" system. But Grant has found it to be a far better long-term indicator of the coming trend in bond prices than the public pronouncements of the "experts."

210   Part 4: *Spreads*

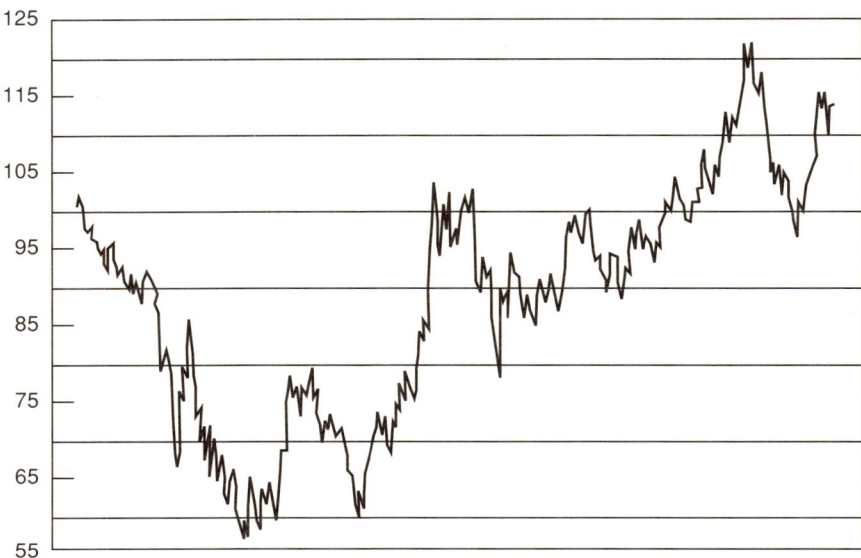

U.S. Bonds, Weekly Futures Close, 11/4/77 to 9/8/95

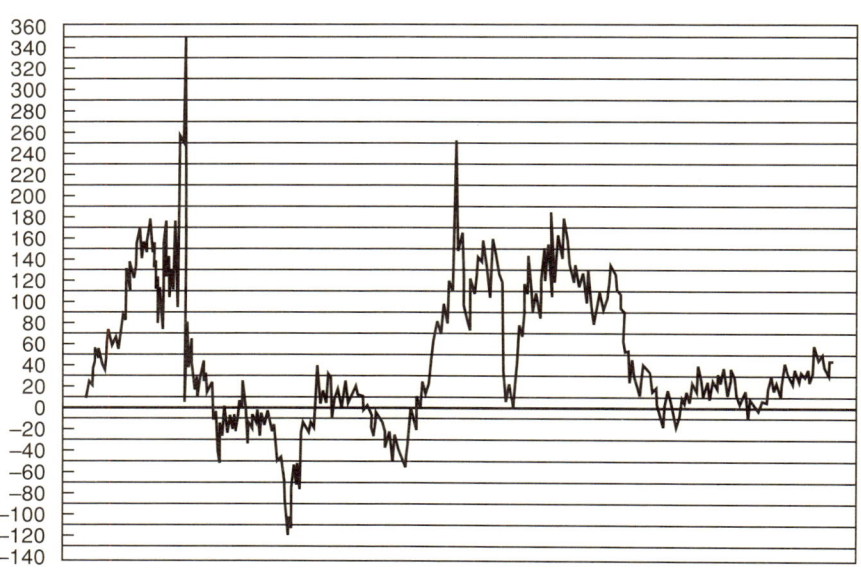

Platinum/Gold Spread, Weekly Closes, Closest U.S. Futures, 11/4/77 to 9/8/95

Spread 26: *The Platinum/Gold Spread Indicator for Bonds* 211

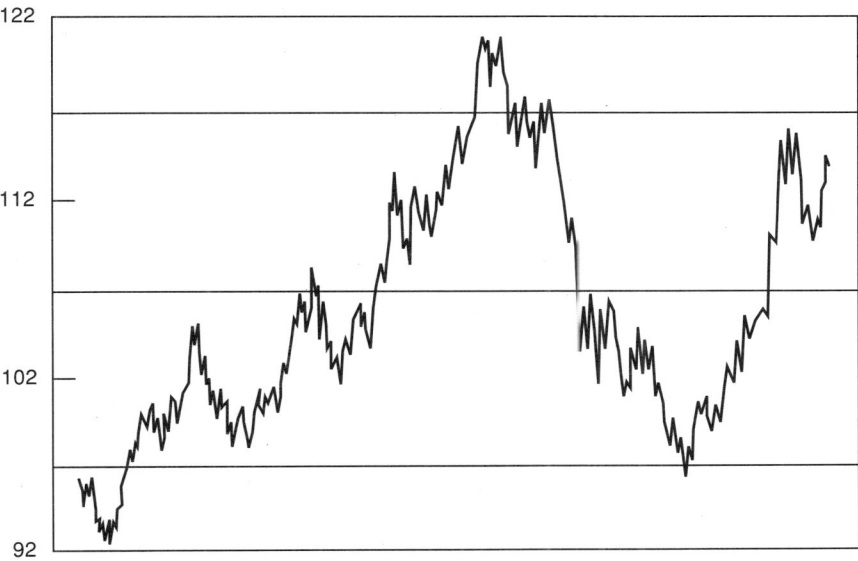

U.S. Bond Futures, Daily Closes, 5/6/91 to 9/8/95

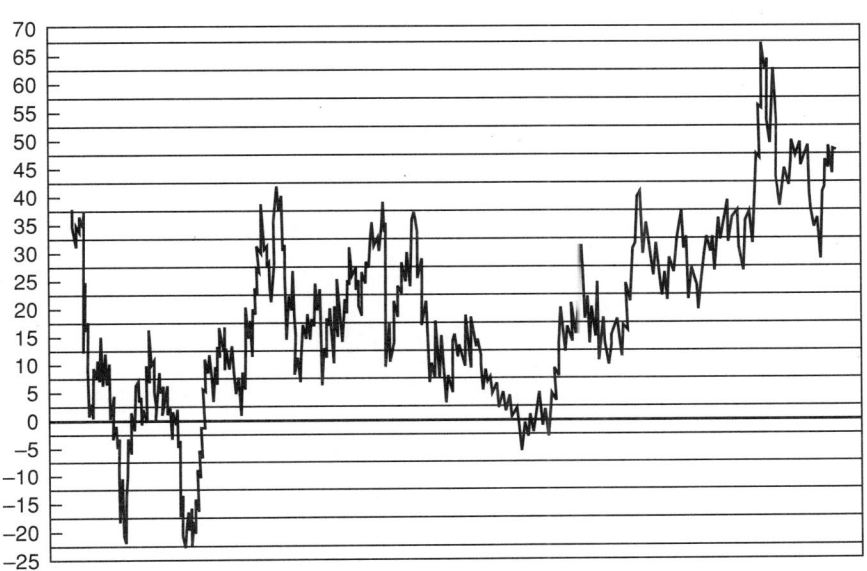

Platinum/Gold Spread, Oct./Oct. & April/April U.S. futures, Daily Closes 5/6/91 to 9/8/95

Spread 27

Well-Known Spread Charts

The following are "compressed" well-known spread charts that cover nearly 20 years of data.

The tip is to buy during those months when the spread is at the lower end of the chart. The trap to avoid is using a seasonal trap blindly without checking how the spread compares to the 20-year history.

Phil Tiger is the known expert in spread history. He's with Smith Barney.

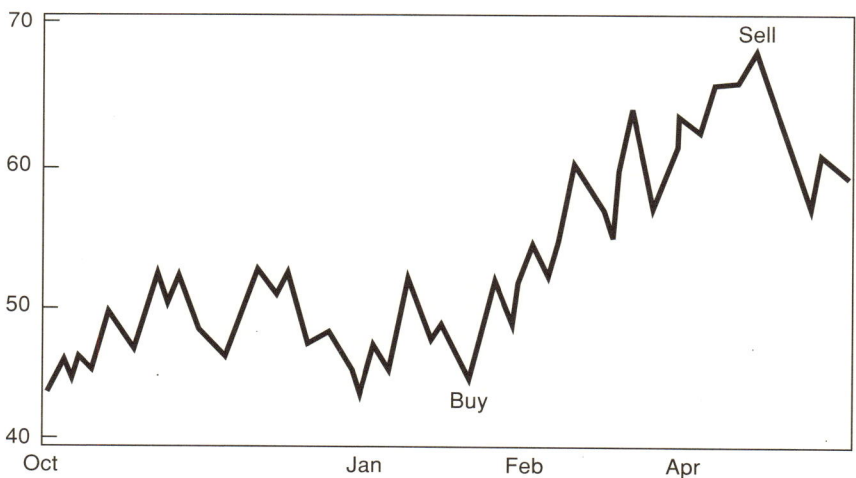

May CBOT Corn Minus May CBOT Wheat
Analysis from 1973 through 1994

Call the Chicago Board of Trade at 312-435-3500 and ask for a free Booklet on this Spread. *(Tell them Neal sent you.)*

Spread 27: *Well-Known Spread Charts* 213

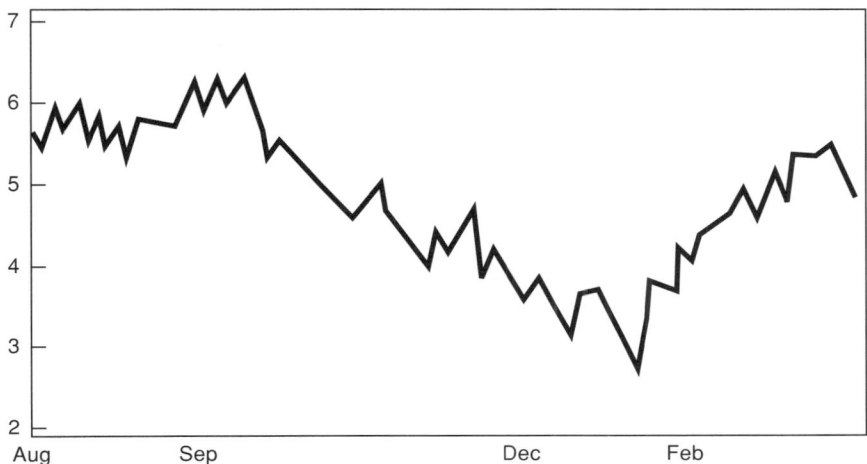

Look for bottom action into the New Year.

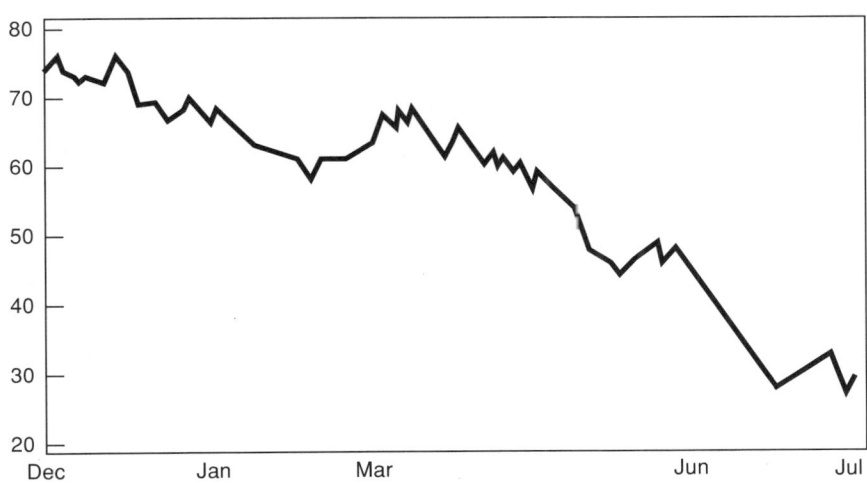

Very volatile spread. Don't wait much past April.

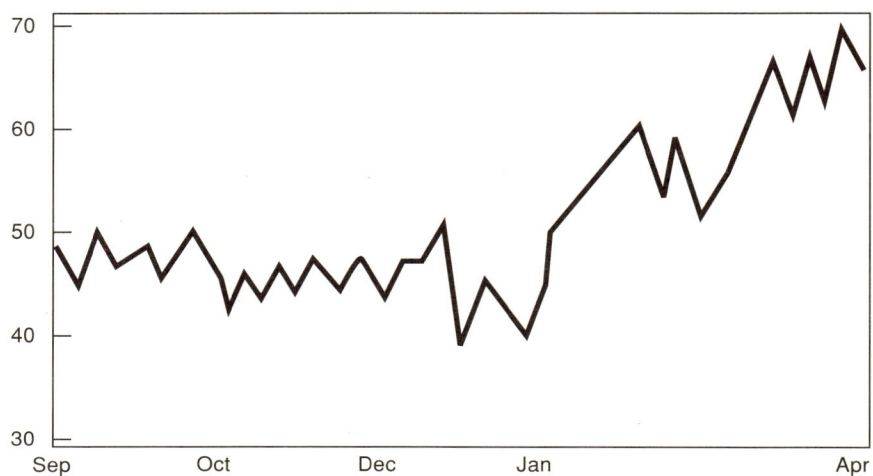

Trade this one with close stops.

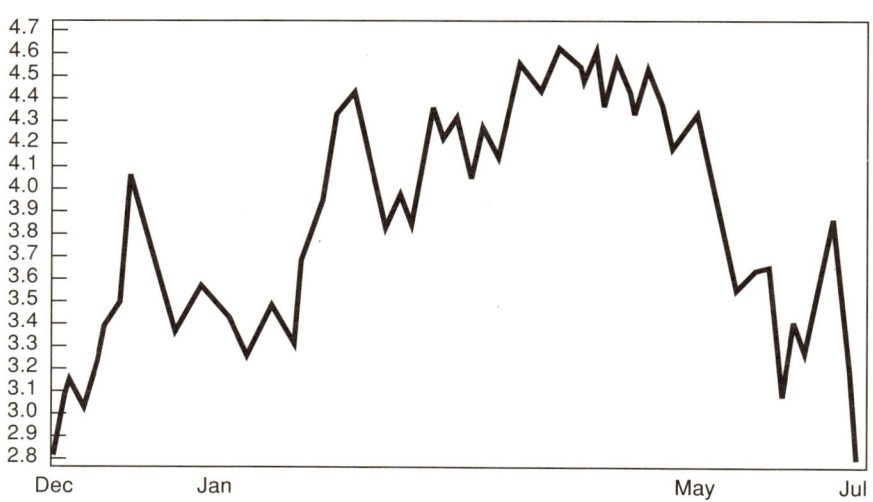

This spread should be traded by those who have strong knowledge of fundamentals.

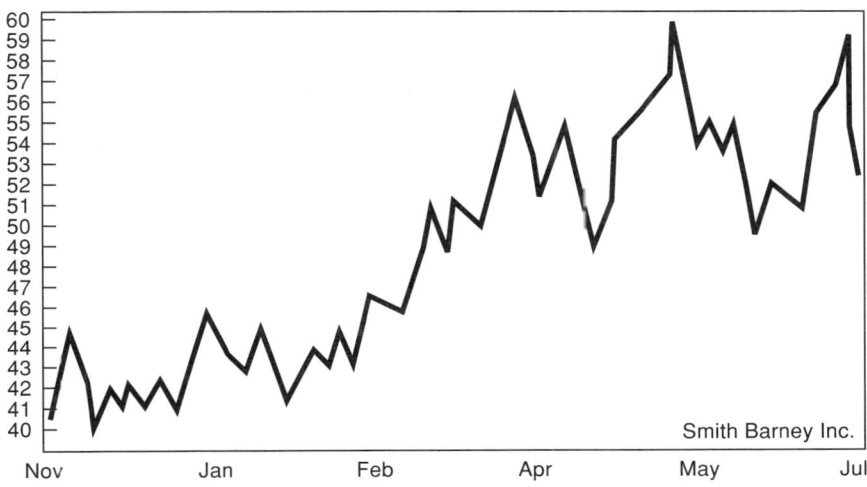

An old favorite. But I lost money trading it. Never double up on this spread. 100 points of "heat" is plenty.

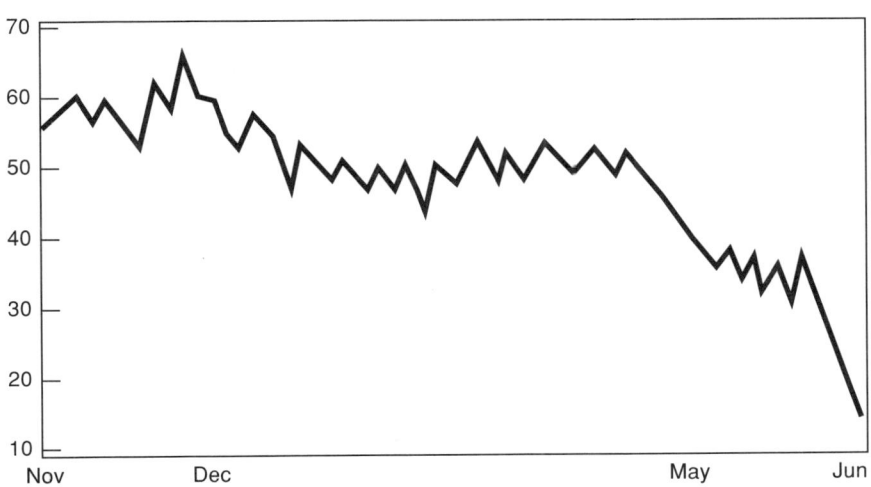

Use a 23-day moving average before trading.

Part 4: Spreads

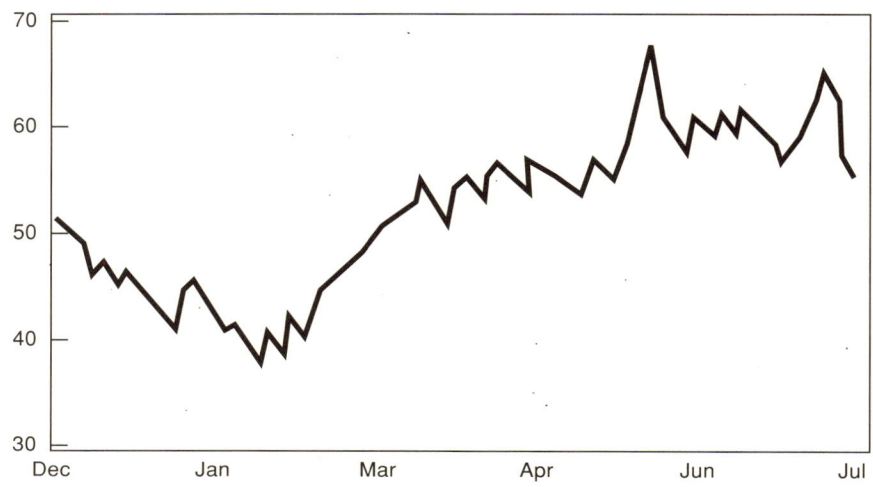

This is weather related, but if it goes against you for three days . . . bye-bye!

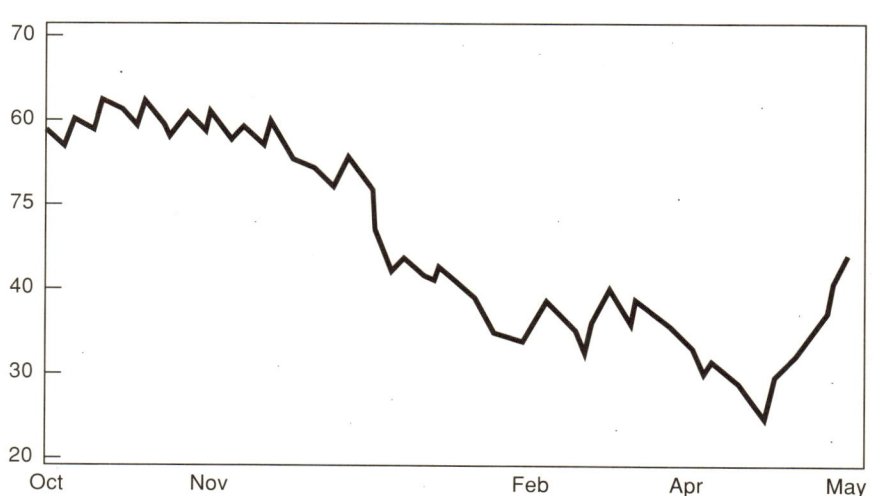

This one has a tendency to trend. Watch for extremes.

Part 5

Tales from the Trenches

These "Tales from the Trenches" are anecdotes about the exchanges and their traders. The sometimes entertaining and colorful stories are meant to give you another insight into the minds of the professional floor traders.

Author Frank Norris described in *The Pit: A Story of Chicago* (New York: Penguin Books, 1994.) an opening in the wheat pit in the early 1900s. He wrote:

> *Instantly tumult was unchained. Arms were flung upward in strenuous gestures, and from above the crowding heads in the*

Wheat Pit a multitude of hands, eager, ten fingers extended, leaped into the air. All articulate expression was lost in the single explosion of sound as the traders surged downwards to the center of the Pit, grabbing each other, struggling towards each other, tramping, stamping, charging through with might and main.

In all these years not much has really changed. What is it like for me when I walk into the pit? Well, for the last few months I have been coming in after the opening, so it usually starts like this:

"Hey, Bug Man is here. Finally got out of bed."

"One-half offered, do you want to trade or what?" says a trader. "Did you hear me, one-half offered."

"Hey, Neal, are we above the Pivot? Because I have all you want at three quarters."

"Hey, Sam, ask Neal if he likes your Gucci shoes."

"Nice shoes, Sam," I remark.

"They're bogus, man, they are plastic. I bought them at Payless."

"Well, if it rains, you're in luck," I reply.

"Rain, did someone say rain?" a booming voice comes from the back of the pit.

"What rain?" I ask.

"You said rain, and if it's not raining I'll report you to Investigation and Audit for starting a rumor," says another pit scalper.

"Hey, man, maybe you're mixing up brain and rain," I remark in frustration.

The seconds turn into minutes and the banter turns to chaos when a new price level is reached. The same guys who kidded me are now out to pick my pockets. In a moment of exasperation, I remark to the broker, "I swear these traders would slice their mom's throat for a tick."

"What do you mean, *would* cut their mother's throat?" says the broker.

Most of these guys already have.

Traders are always told that eventually there is a light at the end of the trading tunnel. After scalping in the Currency Pit for three years, a local trader hung up a sign at his clearing firm that read: "Due to economic conditions, the light at the end of the tunnel has been turned off."

F.U.D., a currency broker, always reminds me of the time the entire three-month range of the British Pound Futures was taken out within seven minutes. "Customers were filled one thousand points away on some of their stops."

"My goodness," I remarked. "The customers must have been upset."

"No," he said. "The customers understood, but it was actually the locals who thought they should have received more of the paper."

It is not uncommon to watch a trader lose a million dollars in one day and eventually come back. Of course, getting another clearing firm to sponsor you is another matter.

"How can you tell when your commodity broker is lying?"

"His lips are moving."

The one great thing about trading is that nobody will stab you in the back. They usually stab you in the front.

Trading is similar to building a bowling alley in your brain and then spending good money to throw gutter balls.

Barry and Ben were trading partners. Barry always knew when to buy and Ben always knew when the perfect time came to sell. During the stock market crash of 1987, Ben took that day off. In fact, Ben took the next two years off.

At the posh East Bank Club many traders work out at the end of the day. You can always tell the nouveau riche traders. Ask them what time it is and they say, "My Rolex says 4:00 P.M." Ask where their car is parked and they say, "My Porsche is in the garage." Ask about their workout and they say, "My personal trainer says I am not fat, just too short for my weight."

And who can forget the trader who got a clerk to wear a disguise and give an order to a broker. The reason: If the order was a winner, the trader would claim it as his. And if the trader was a loser, the clerk would never be found. Yes, they were caught and prosecuted.

Imagine walking into a place of work and seeing people eating sunflower seeds, chewing gum, throwing paper airplanes, and joking around. Sound like a typical Chicago high school? It's just the typical pit on a slow day around 10:30 A.M.

And, if there is a disease that can be airborne, you can bet your next cold will travel from pit to pit.

She walked onto the trading floor and she was beautiful in body, mind, and spirit. She actually stopped the trading as she walked by each pit at the exchange. But as she passed, the traders looked the other way and would not make eye contact.

Who was this woman who attracted men in one second and repelled them in the next? As I finally caught up with her, she turned to notice me. I found the attraction overwhelming—that is, until I noticed the badge on her purse strap. It said in big bold letters, **C.F.T.C.** I don't care how beautiful you are, the C.F.T.C. (Commodity Futures Trading Commission) is to traders what Kryptonite is to Superman.

Many of the traders who attend my Computer Training for Traders have attended basic trading schools and hyped "Rags to Riches" courses like Ken Roberts and like Joe Ross Seminars. Once a student asked if he should take my course. I suggested that he should have a basic knowledge of Windows. He called back and said that I insulted him.

"Even a five-year-old child has a knowledge of windows," he stated.

"I meant the software program."

He replied, "If software were so important, my other teachers would have supplied me with it."

One trader said that he had been praying to Ceres, the goddess of grain and eating at her restaurant at the CBOT, and hoping for good fortune. He had lost money for 63 consecutive weeks. His wife had left him and his clearing firm was about to pull his seat.

"Why me?" he cried. "Why me?"

A voice boomed over his head from a female trader, "Women hate a crybaby, especially when they are a goddess."

There's an old saying, "A trader will hit the pit floor before the deck he is holding will." All this means is that filling paper for various trading houses is such a plum position that local traders will let a trader hit the ground and try to get his deck. Are we insensitive or what?

Then there was the time a floor broker was supposed to buy 150 gold contracts, and he even confirmed the fact that the gold was purchased. When the customer complained, the broker was baffled.

"What's the problem?" said the broker.

"I said 150 not 15."

And sure enough, the order said 150. But how did the broker let that happen. Simple. The order clerk wrote the order so small that the broker's thumb covered the zero in 150 and so it was read as 15.

The bottom line: The broker to this day is still paying off the customer.

The trader came bursting out of the men's restroom and cried, "There are pay toilets in the men's room." We had no idea what he was saying until he finished his sentence.

"I just went to the bathroom for five minutes and my position went $3,500 against me."

Trader Tim Henry tells me about the last trade he made. His advisor told him to buy on a buy stop above a Bollinger Band. And sell on a stop just below a Bollinger Band. Tim was trading S&Ps. So first the market hit his buy stop and then raced down and got the sell stop. Ouch! Well, so much for Mr. Bollinger.

Don Small, a former Soymeal Broker and current trader in Crop Insurance, tells me about the former Chicago cop in the pit who still carries a handgun under his trading jacket. The first time I wasn't sure, the second time no doubt. Do you think Don ever argued with this guy? By the way, no guns are allowed on the floor.

A university professor once asked me for the names of traders that could be used in some social experiments dealing with tension and stress.

"I thought you guys used rats for that type of experiment."

"We do," he remarked, "but, after a while, you kind of get attached to those rodents."

He certainly wouldn't have any attachment problems with the pit traders I know.

It's a fact, the reason traders wear clear glasses is to avoid sharp blows to the eyes and to avoid the splat of flying spit balls.

Then there was the trader who had to prove Chicago pizza was better than New York's, so he gave his clerk a first-class airfare ticket and told the clerk to be on the next flight to the Big Apple. The total cost of the pizza, $859.98. But the comparison was called off when the clerk came back with a thin-crust pizza. How could he make such a mistake? Chicago is known for thick pizza. Yes, the clerk lost his job.

Traders who smoke quality cigars can be found at Jack Schwartz in the Insurance Exchange Building or at Rubovitz in the lobby of the Chicago Board of Trade. This is where you will usually find the high rollers. Overheard over a Dunhill cigar:

> "The stock market has nothing to do with the President," said the S&P local.
>
> "People didn't say that when Reagan was President. They used to call it Reaganomics," replied the Eurodollar trader.
>
> "Maybe you would like your Democratic butt kicked, too," the local said.
>
> "Try it now," said the trader.

And with that the broker took the cigar butt out of the trader's mouth and kicked it across the room. They both fell down laughing in the humidor.

In many sports one is ranked by other professionals. Many times traders rank each other when they are in the pit. While there is no ranking, the following guide is how traders sometimes describe each other in the trading trenches. I have done my best to figure what they mean. Where would you rank yourself?

Rating

0.0 ***Pie in the sky dreams and unrealistic expectations.***

> Usually a victim of commodity seminars. Or a follower of (i.e., Ken Roberts) some guru (you will learn to trade or "trade with our money"). Or purchased a system with simulated track record. Or blindly follows broker's recommendations without question. Fails because of low trading capital. Gives power of attorney to broker without understanding risks.

1.0 ***The trader has just started to trade. Still should practice.***

> Trader is just trying to stay in the game, not make money. Believes "day trading" means you trade everyday. Wrong!

Rating

1.5 ***The trader has limited experience and is still trying to card trades.***

Spends time reading books, not trading. Crucial that trader trades and stops looking for Grail. Trader still has trouble knowing what is a good trade. Understands risk management or at least the basics of staying "in the game." Uses too many technical indicators. Should be assigned to senior trader for tutoring. Trader is getting less emotional and more cognitive about trades. Still loses temper or is easily shaken up by other traders. Shows promise.

2.0 ***The trader feels comfortable in the pit but needs more experience.***

Few out-trades. Knows people in the pit. Still needs to focus on order flow. Forgets when reports come out and still gets caught off guard. Less emotional.

2.5 ***Dependable trader.***

Is learning to judge where the market is going. Still caught off guard by sudden market moves.

3.0 ***Fair trader but does not know when to increase size or scale back in position.***

Every once in a while takes wild chances.

4.0 ***More dependable.***

Trader knows spreads, options, and when to use them. Knows reports are coming out. Watches back months, too.

4.5 ***Trader is developing good market anticipation.***

Does not wait for the market to move but moves with it.

Rating

4.6 ***Trader has begun to master the intricacies of the market.***

Understands the difference between off and on the floor trading. Floor brokers count on him for decent size.

4.7 ***Respected in pit.***

Trader can successfully execute any type of trade and uses money management skills. Is sought after by other firms. Taking the other side of any trade is no problem. Asked to serve on exchange committees.

4.8 ***Parade time.***

Trader is asked to manage money or become a Commodity Trading Advisor.

Floor Traders Unabashed Glossary

This is unofficial and reflects more of floor trader attitude than reality.

Arbitrage The simultaneous purchase and sale of identical or equivalent financial instruments or commodity futures in order to benefit from a discrepancy in their price relationship. Not for use by the public.

Auction Market Phrase used to explain market movement. Not tradeable. Great seminar hype.

Back Months The futures of options on futures months being traded that are furthest from expiration. May lack liquidity so be careful.

Bear One who believes prices will move lower and acts on it or wishes he had.

Bear Market A market in which prices are declining, usually for two weeks, or two years.

Bid The price that the market participants are willing to pay. But the public must pay the offer. Sorry Folks.

Booze Cheap drinks. Usually consumed by clerks on Friday. Usually combined with free eats or nickel beers.

Bull One who expects prices to rise. Usually an optimist.

Bull Market A market in which prices are rising, need a month to confirm.

Buy on Close To buy at the end of a trading session at a price within the closing range. Expect a "terrible" price.

Buy on Opening To buy at the beginning of a trading session at a price within the opening range. Public gets the high end. Wrong time to enter market.

CFTC The Commodity Futures Trading Commission as created by the Commodity Futures Trading Commission Act of 1974. This government agency currently regulates the nation's commodity futures industry. Federal cutbacks will hurt the public.

Call An option to buy a commodity, security, or futures con-tract at a specified price anytime between now and the expiration date of the option contract. Best purchased when volatility is low.

Camp A summer place to send children, not trade.

Cash Commodity The actual physical commodity as distinguished from a futures commodity. Prices not easily accessible to public.

Chart Services Combined with a telephone hotline usually means disaster for public traders.

Close, The The period at the end of the trading session. Sometimes used to refer to the closing range. Can be very wide at times.

Commission (or Round Turn) The one-time fee charged by a broker to a customer when a futures or options on futures position is liquidated. There is no relationship between commission charged and service once you get past $50.00.

Contract Month The month in which futures contracts may be satisfied by making or accepting delivery. Usually the worst place to be if you are the public.

Day Trading Refers to establishing and liquidating the same position or positions within one day's trading, thus ending the day with no established position in the market. Impossible without low commission and floor access. Real time quotes needed, too.

Dream Team The same old seminar hustlers joined together as a group.

Elliott Wave Some great ideas. Long-term view needed.

Fines Court actions or decisions against an individual. Ask if you don't know.

Floor Broker An exchange member who is paid a fee for executing orders for Clearing Members or their customers. A very sweet deal for a trader.

Floor Trader An exchange member who generally trades only for his/her own account or for an account controlled by him/her. Also referred to as a "local." They are fast and furious and can change their mind quicker than you can say "over bought."

"Guru" A new breed of market folks who claim great market calls, but can't produce an actual monthly statement.

Hedge The purchase or sale of a futures contract as a temporary substitute to a cash market transaction to be made at a later date. Usually it involves opposite positions in the cash market and futures market at the same time. Rationale why market exists.

Limit Order An order given by a customer that specifies a price; the order can be executed only if the market reaches or betters that price. Seldom used by public, but used by sophisticated traders.

Limit Up As "up as a contract" can go in one day. Also a restaurant at CME.

Liquidation Any transaction that offsets or closes out a long or short futures position. Usually done taking a loss for most traders.

"Loud Mouth" Someone who gives ridiculous bids and offers in the pit. Someone who is obnoxious. It can be a customer or a broker.

Margin Call A demand for additional funds because of adverse price movement. A "wake up" call to leave position.

Market Order An order for immediate execution given to a broker to buy or sell at the best obtainable price. The best price is really what the pit will give you.

Market Profile Another technical tool that explains what already happened.

Maximum Price Fluctuation The amount the contract price can change, up or down, during one trading session.

Minimum Price Fluctuation Smallest increment of price movement possible in trading a given contract, often referred to as a "tick." Those "ticks" add up fast.

M.I.T. Market-If-Touched. A price order that automatically becomes a market order if the price is reached. Not accepted by all exchanges.

Nearby The nearest active trading month of a futures or options on futures contract. Also referred to a "lead month." Be sure "lead month" is also top step.

Offer Indicates a willingness to sell a futures contract at a given price. Floor does this easier than public.

Open Interest total number of futures or options on futures contracts that have not yet been offset or fulfilled by delivery. Great way to check the worth of a contract.

Open Order An order to a broker that is good until it is canceled or executed. Many times forgotten by a trader.

Opening Price (or Range) The range of prices at which the first bids and offers were made or first transactions were completed. The high or low of the day is usually made at the opening.

Out-Trades When there is some confusion or error on a trade. This is a nightmare for "locals."

Position An interest in the market, either long or short, in the form of open contracts. (*See* **Open Interest**.)

Premium (This has two definitions.) (1) The excess of one futures contract price over that of another, or over the cash market price. (2) The dollar amount agreed upon between the pur-chaser and seller for the purchase or sale of a futures option—purchasers pay the premium and sellers (writers) receive the premium.
  1. Used in spreads.
  2. Used in options.

Radio Boys People who call promising great returns on options. Found on AM radio.

Rally An upward movement of prices following a steep decline.

Range The high and low prices or high and low offers, recorded during a specified time. Used for calculating many technical indicators.

Reaction A decline in prices following a steady advance. The opposite of rally. Also, what happens when you lose.

Research Most misunderstood aspect of trading. Many firms no longer produce research, just repackage or buy from outside. Do your own.

Rhythm of the Market One-Two-Cha-Cha-Cha. Blame It on the Bossa Nova. Let's Twist Again. It Takes Two to Tango. Traders can spend a lifetime trying to figure it out. Practice dancing.

Scalp To trade for small gains. Scalping normally involves establishing and liquidating a position quickly. Public will scalp a profit, but not a losing trade.

Seasonals Usually found on the table with salt and pepper. Also a type of trading and broken down to almost "sure thing" trading. Best to use in the money options and stay away from futures.

Settlement Price A figure determined by the closing range that is used to calculate gains and losses in futures market accounts. How winners and losers keep score.

Shmooze Courting floor broker, so locals get market orders.

Short One who has sold a futures contract to establish mar-ket position. Tends to be commercials or big traders on the "short" side.

Speculator One who attempts to trade price changes through buying and selling futures contracts; aims to make profits; does not use the futures market in connection with the production, processing, marketing, or handling of a product. But the more they know about the production, proces-sing, etc., the more successful they will be.

Summer Intern A person with great connections so they obtain summer employment.

Turtle A group of traders that forgot to copyright the name so other members exploit it for seminar circuit. Also, what you keep as a pet.

Zinger The unexpected shock to the market that you forgot to prepare for. Other words may explain this concept, too, but are considered "swearing."

About the Author

NEAL T. WEINTRAUB is an educator and trader specializing in analyzing the markets with various software packages. He is the founder of the Center for Advanced Research in Computerized Trading and offers seminars on day trading and international hedging. His book *The Weintraub Day Trader* is the basis of most day trading concepts. Neal teaches Fundamental Analysis, Spread Trading, and Computer Applications of CME markets for the Chicago Mercantile Exchange. Most of his students are professional floor personnel and career-oriented traders. In addition, Neal was on staff of the Chicago Board of Trade, where he was instrumental in introducing the highly successful Bond Options contract. The financial press has recognized Neal's prowess and *The Wall Street Journal* has featured his Pivot Point technique and he is frequently quoted in the trade press for his unorthodox views of the markets. Neal has brought a marketing orientation to trading based on his work experience with MTV, Panasonic, The Disney Channel, and Warner Communications. Neal currently clears his trades through Goldenberg and Hehmeyer at the Chicago Board of Trade and is a pit trader (local) as well as an off-the-floor computer trader.

For information on seminars, software, and computer courses, write: 8815 Ewing, Evanston, Illinois 60203. ■

Thank you for choosing Irwin Professional Publishing for your business information needs. If you are part of a corporation, professional association, or government agency, consider our newest option: Irwin Professional Custom Publishing. This allows you to create customized books, manuals, and other materials from your organization's resources, select chapters of our books, or both.

Irwin Professional Publishing books are also excellent resources for training/educational programs, premiums, and incentives. For information on volume discounts or Custom Publishing, call 1-800-634-3966.

Other books of interest to you from Irwin Professional Publishing . . .

CURTIS ARNOLD'S PPS TRADING SYSTEM
A Proven Method for Consistently Beating the Market
Curtis M. Arnold

Since its introduction in 1989, the Pattern Probability System has received rave reviews. This book reveals everything which has made it such a huge success from the system's underlying principles to trade selection criteria to money management.

1-55738-877-6   225 pages

THE HANDBOOK OF TECHNICAL ANALYSIS
A Comprehensive Guide to Analytical Methods, Trading Systems, and Technical Indicators
Darrell R. Jobman, Editor

"Darrell Jobman is one of the 'know it alls' of the industry—he knows technical analysis, he knows trading, he knows systems, he knows everything having to do with futures trading."

Ginger Szala
Editor, Futures magazine

1-55738-597-1   400 pages

INVESTMENT SECRETS OF A HEDGE FUND MANAGER
Exploiting the Herd Mentality of the Financial Markets
Laurence A. Connors and Blake E. Hayward

Gives a host of proven strategies to trade the stock, futures, and options markets. Simple and easy-to-use, the strategies are designed to take advantage of the herd mentality of the financial markets and the tendency of the majority of investors to panic at identifiable moments. Clear, hard-headed, and realistic.

1-55738-900-4   250 pages

(Continued)

THE OPTION'S COURSE
A Winning Program for Investors and Traders
Rudi Binnewies

Covers everything from option fundamentals to complex strategies and functions as both a self-teaching tool and as a reference to virtually every approach and tactic used in the options market.
1-55738-871-7   300 pages